Spanish

Margaret Barca

Contents

Introduction

Fresh, simple, regional, seasonal — these qualities are at the heart of classic Spanish food. While 'new wave' Spanish cooking is often startlingly inventive, for most day-to-day meals traditional dishes still prevail. Vegetables, eggs, olive oil, fresh and cured meats — including the paprika-spiked sausage chorizo, the country's renowned ham (*jamon*) and salted cod (*bacalao*) — are just some of the time-honored produce that is central to Spain's varied cuisines.

The Spanish love their food and they love sharing it — be it the snack-sized morsels known as tapas, or larger dishes such as paella, perfect for special occasions. Variety and flexibility are key: you can size up tapas to make a meal or divide larger dishes to serve as snacks. The Spanish appetite isn't about size — it's about the love of good food, and of authentic flavors derived from local produce and regional traditions.

This book provides an easy-to-follow introduction to the classic flavors that are intrinsic to Spain's cuisine.

Spanish Basics

The cuisine of Spain is rich with heritage, acknowledging influences from the Arab world and the Americas; as well as traditional peasant life, the bounty of the surrounding seas, the relatively equable Mediterranean climate, and the harsher conditions and landscape of some inland regions. In the north, French customs emerge in the hearty, long-braised dishes of beans and cured sausage. Further south, in Andalusia in particular, the use of saffron and other spices, figs, oranges and nuts are a tangible reminder of Moorish influences.

A few distinctive ingredients permeate typical Spanish cuisine. Including some of these in your cooking will help capture the true flavors of Spain.

All varieties of anchovies are widely used in Spanish cooking. The most familiar are the pinkish-brown variety, which are salt-cured and then canned or bottled in oil. A Mediterranean specialty, increasingly available in the US, are 'white' anchovies, known as *boquerones*. These are simply filleted anchovies marinated in vinegar, which gives them a softer texture and a more subtle flavor.

Dried salt cod (*bacalao*) looks unpromising: large, slightly curled slabs of pale dried fish usually encrusted with salt. But once it has been soaked and cooked, you will understand why it is such a favorite ingredient in Spanish cooking. To prepare, rinse well, place in a bowl, cover with cold water and leave in the refrigerator for 48 hours. (Change the water twice a day to remove excess salt and rehydrate the fish.) Drain, and rinse again. It is now ready to be cooked.

Meats such as the spicy, sometimes fiery, chorizo sausage and jamon (pronounced 'ha-mon'), a dry-cured ham cut in wafer-thin slices, are other much used ingredients. Jamon comes in different grades but all are delicious: jamon Iberico is one of Spain's most famous exports, however jamon scrrano is less expensive and is a fine substitute. If you can't find jamon, use Italian prosciutto, or a smoked ham, instead.

Morcilla, the Spanish version of blood sausage or black pudding, consists of pigs' blood, onion and rice, with spices (notably pimenton). It is frequently served as a tapa, thickly sliced and lightly fried; it is also a frequent addition to soups and stews.

Spanish wine has enjoyed a rise in international recognition and popularity, and none more so than sherry — or Jerez — named after the town where this fortified wine has been produced for many centuries. Sherry can range from the very pale, dry, fino sherries, to the darker, sweeter (and higher in alcohol) oloroso styles. One of the most sought-after sherries is Pedro Ximenez, sometimes known just as PX — a dark, luscious sweet sherry made from the sun-dried Pedro Ximenez grape variety. Use PX to enrich slow-cooked meat dishes, or as the perfect complement to creamy Spanish desserts and cakes.

Spain is renowned for its olive oil. More than 200 olive varieties are grown and the country is the world's largest exporter of olive oil. Like all Mediterranean nations, the

Spanish use olive oil liberally in their cooking. It is common to drizzle a little (or a lot!) onto any savory dish, and it is baked into cakes and biscuits and, of course, used extensively for frying. Rich and fruity extra-virgin olive oil is especially good for eating with bread, salads, vegetables and soups.

Various small, mild pimientos (chili peppers) are used — both fresh and preserved — in many Spanish dishes. Popular varieties include piquillo and padron and they are added to salads and tortillas, stuffed with tuna or salted cod, or roasted over coals, drizzled with oil and offered as simple tapas.

Spanish paprika (pimenton) is a staple ingredient in Spanish cooking. Made from red pimientos which have been smoked and ground, Spanish paprika is available in sweet (dulce), mild (agridulce) and hot (picante) varieties. Spanish paprika is quite different to the Hungarian style more commonly available in the US, due to its distinctive smoky flavor. You can substitute smoked paprika, if the Spanish variety can't be found.

The Moors brought saffron to Spain more than a thousand years ago and today, Spain is the world's largest producer of the spice. Saffron's subtle fragrance and vibrant color is integral to many Spanish dishes — particularly seafood — and gives paella its rich golden hue.

Aromatic, with complex flavors, true Spanish sherry vinegar (Vinagre de Jerez) — made from sherry produced in the Jerez region of southern Spain — adds a distinctive taste to dressings, sauces and soups.

Spaniards love shellfish. Scrub mussel and clam shells and rinse under cold running water. To debeard mussels, pull off the tuft of bristly hairs at the junction of the shells. Tap any shells that are slightly open; if they don't close immediately, discard. After cooking, discard any shells that do not open up.

Freshly caught octopus can be tough and rubbery, and requires tenderizing before being cooked. Check with your fish retailer – often octopus sold retail has already been tenderized. To prepare the octopus, use a sharp knife to cut the head from the tentacles below the hard beak. Push the beak up and out, then discard. Turn the body inside-out and remove all internal organs and the ink sac. Use the knife to slice away the eye. Rinse well.

The Spanish often keep the tails when cooking prawns, so check the recipe before following these instructions. Remove the legs and head, and then peel off the shell, including the tail. Use a sharp knife to make an incision along the back and remove the digestive tract.

Squid and **calamari** are widely used in Spanish cooking. The smaller they are, the more tender. To prepare, put the seafood into a sink of cold water and rinse well. Pull the tentacles away from the hood tube (the innards should come with them), cut to sever. Rinse tentacles and set aside. Grasp the transparent spine inside the hood and pull it out. Rinse the hood until clean, then peel off the thin, colored layer of skin and discard.

There is more information on Spanish ingredients on page 248.

While you don't need any special dishes to cook Spanish food, you may decide to invest in these for an authentic effect.

Cazuela — a glazed terracotta dish which comes in various shapes and sizes, used for both cooking and serving Spanish food. It is fired to a very high density and retain heat well. Cazuelas are available from many cookware stores. When using a cazuela over direct heat, it is best to use a heat diffuser.

Paellera (often simply called a paella pan) — a large, round, shallow pan, (traditionally cast-iron with two handles), designed for cooking and serving paella. The width allows more surface area for the crisp crust (socarrat) which should develop on the bottom of good paella. If you can't find a paellera, substitute a large, medium-weight (this helps the rice cook evenly) frying pan will do instead.

Tapas

As one version of the story goes, a *tapa* (the word literally means 'cover' or 'lid') was a piece of bread placed over a glass of wine by workers in the field to keep insects away. Later, it became the custom to add some ham or cheese to the bread, to be served as a snack with a drink.

Today tapas can be anything from a simple bowl of olives, spicy little empanadas stuffed with tuna, or a cazuela of sizzling prawns, heady with the fragrance of garlic. These morsels are the perfect accompaniment to a chilled sherry, a Spanish beer or light red wine. Or you can serve several tapas as a starter, or larger quantities (raciones) together to make a meal.

❮ ARTICHOKE & JAMON EMPANADAS (PAGE 12)

Artichoke & Jamon Empanadas

SERVES 4

5 ounces marinated
artichokes, drained and
roughly chopped
2 ounces jamon (or
prosciutto), chopped

4 ounces Swiss cheese, grated
1 egg, separated,
yolks lightly beaten
freshly ground black pepper
9 ounces ready-rolled puff
pastry

Preheat the oven to 425°F. Line two baking sheets with parchment (baking paper).

Mix artichokes in a small bowl with ham, cheese and egg yolk. Season with pepper.

Cut the pastry into 2½-in circles. Spoon a little of the artichoke mixture into the center of each pastry round, fold over to form a semicircle and pinch pastry together to seal. Place on the prepared baking sheets.

Brush empanadas with egg white. Place in preheated oven and bake for 20 minutes. Serve hot.

✖ Empanadas are stuffed, baked or fried pastries.

Anchovy & Egg Toast
Tostados

MAKES 12 PIECES

12 thick slices bread from
  baguette
2 cloves garlic, halved
3 eggs
2 tablespoons milk
salt and freshly ground black
  pepper

2 tablespoons extra-virgin
  olive oil
6–8 anchovies in oil, well
  drained and chopped
2 tablespoons baby capers,
  drained

Toast the bread slices until just golden. Rub cut garlic over toasted bread slices.

Lightly whisk the eggs with the milk and season with salt and pepper.

Heat 1 tablespoon of the olive oil in a non-stick pan over low heat. Add egg mixture and cook, stirring, until almost scrambled but still creamy. Stir in the anchovy pieces.

Pile scrambled egg onto the bread slices, drizzle with a little olive oil and scatter with capers. Serve immediately.

※ Tostados are toasted or are made from a toasted ingredient.

Asparagus with Scrambled Eggs

SERVES 4

8 spears young asparagus,
  tough ends trimmed
boiling water, to blanch
  asparagus
4 large eggs

1 teaspoon sweet or hot
  Spanish paprika
pinch of salt
3 tablespoons olive oil
1 clove garlic, thinly sliced

Place asparagus in boiling water and blanch for a few minutes, until it starts to soften but is still bright green. Strain and cut into pieces 1-inch long.

Beat the eggs in a bowl with paprika and salt.

Heat the olive oil in a non-stick fry pan over medium heat. Add garlic and fry for 1 minute, then add asparagus pieces and sauté for an additional minute. Add beaten eggs to the pan and cook over low heat an additional minute, stirring all the time, until eggs are almost set.

Remove from heat (the eggs will continue to cook, but should stay creamy) and serve immediately.

✕ You can serve this tapa in small bowls or piled onto toasted bread slices. Choose small young asparagus spears (traditionally wild asparagus is used).

Broad Beans with Jamon

SERVES 4–6

1 tablespoon olive oil
1 clove garlic, crushed
½ red onion, finely chopped
6½ ounces jamon (or
   prosciutto), roughly
   chopped
2 tablespoons dry sherry

3 cups shelled broad beans,
   fresh or frozen
½ cup chicken or vegetable
   stock
salt and freshly ground black
   pepper

Heat the olive oil in a non-stick fry pan over medium heat. Add garlic and onion, and sauté for 3–4 minutes until softened. Add ham and sauté for another 3–4 minutes. Pour sherry into pan and cook until absorbed. Add the broad beans and stock, stirring to combine, and bring to a boil. Reduce the heat, cover, and simmer for about 10 minutes.

Check seasoning and add pepper if needed. Serve warm or at room temperature.

✖ Add some sliced hard-boiled eggs and serve with crusty bread for a light lunch.

Baked Garlic Mushroom Caps

4 tablespoons butter, melted
2 tablespoons olive oil
1 cup fresh breadcrumbs
½ cup chopped garlic chives

salt and freshly ground black
  pepper
2 pounds 3 ounces button
  mushrooms, stems removed

Preheat oven to 350°F.

Mix butter, olive oil, breadcrumbs and chives in a bowl, and season with salt and pepper, to taste.

Spoon the breadcrumb mix into the mushroom caps, pressing it down well. Place mushrooms on a non-stick baking sheet, put in preheated oven and bake for about 10 minutes, until topping is golden and crisp. Serve warm or at room temperature.

Empanadillas with Tuna

SERVES 4

2 tablespoons olive oil

1 tablespoon chopped onion

1 (3½-ounces) canned tuna
  in water, drained and flaked

2 tablespoons sliced,
  pimento-stuffed olives

½ teaspoon sweet Spanish
  paprika

1 tablespoon finely chopped
  fresh flat-leaf parsley

salt and freshly ground black
  pepper

9 ounces pre-rolled, read-to-
  bake pastry

1 egg yolk, beaten, to glaze

Heat olive oil in a non-stick pan over medium heat. Add onion and cook for 4–5 minutes, stirring occasionally, until softened. Add tuna, olives, paprika and parsley; then cook, stirring, for about 5 minutes. Check seasoning and add salt and pepper if needed. Let cool.

Preheat the oven to 375°F. Line two baking sheets with parchment (baking) paper.

Cut pastry into 3-inch circles and arrange on baking sheets. Place a teaspoon of the tuna mixture on each round and fold the pastry over to form a crescent shape. Press the edges with a fork, or pinch together with your finger, to seal. Brush the tops with beaten egg yolk, and bake in preheated oven for 12–15 minutes, until golden brown. Serve warm.

✕ Empanadillas are little empanadas.

Salt Cod Purée
Brandada de bacalao

SERVES 4–6

1 pound 2 ounces salt cod,
  soaked (see page 4)
2 cups milk
4 black peppercorns
2 sprigs fresh parsley
2 bay leaves
water, to cover cod
2 cloves garlic, chopped
juice of 1 lemon

1 cup olive oil
1 pound 10 ounces potatoes,
  boiled and mashed
3 tablespoons chopped flat-leaf
  parsley
freshly ground black pepper
crisp toasted bread slices or
  piquillo peppers, for serving

Place soaked cod in a large saucepan with the milk, peppercorns, parsley, bay leaves and enough water to cover. Poach gently for 15–20 minutes or until the fish is soft and flaky. Reserve about 3 tablespoons of the poaching liquid. Remove fish carefully from the pan, flake fish and discard bones and skin (make sure there are no small bones left). Put fish into a blender or food processor with garlic and lemon juice. Drizzle in the olive oil and pulse until you have a thick purée. Add potatoes and parsley, and pulse again until just combined (add a little of the reserved poaching liquid if mixture is too thick – it should be creamy and light). Season with pepper.

Serve at room temperature, piled onto crisp toasted bread slices or as a filling for piquillo (spicy red) peppers. The purée will keep, refrigerated, for 2–3 days.

Fried Squid
Calamares fritos

SERVES 4

1 pound 2 ounces squid tubes, sliced into ³⁄₈-inch rings
1½ cups all-purpose flour
2 teaspoons sweet Spanish paprika
salt and freshly ground black pepper

olive oil for deep-frying
bread cube, for testing oil
2 lemons, cut into wedges, to serve
alioli (page 238), to serve

Pat squid rings dry with paper towel.

Mix flour and paprika in a bowl and season with salt and pepper. Toss squid rings in flour until lightly dusted, shaking off any excess.

Heat the olive oil in a deep, heavy-based saucepan until very hot. To test, drop in a cube of bread – it should sizzle and turn brown within a few seconds.

Add the squid rings, a few at a time, and cook for about 2 minutes, until golden brown. Remove with a slotted spoon and drain on paper towels.

Serve hot, with lemon wedges alongside and alioli for dipping.

✕ Cuttlefish pieces are commonly cooked this way too.

Salt Cod Fritters
Bunuelos de bacalao

SERVES 6

1 pound 2 ounces salt cod,
    soaked (see page 4)
2 cups milk
3 tablespoons olive oil
1 onion, finely chopped
2 cloves garlic, chopped
1 pound 2 ounces potatoes,
    boiled and mashed
2 eggs, beaten

2 tablespoons finely chopped
    fresh flat-leaf parsley
salt and freshly ground black
    pepper
olive oil for frying
lemon wedges, and alioli
    (page 238), to serve

Drain the cod, pat dry, and cut into large pieces.

Heat the milk in a large saucepan or deep fry pan over medium heat. Add the cod, and bring to a boil, reduce the heat and simmer very gently for about 30 minutes, until the fish is soft. Drain, and let cool.

Flake the fish, removing any skin or bones, then mash with a fork.

Heat the olive oil in a fry pan, add onion and garlic, and cook over medium heat for a few minutes until softened.

Put mashed potato in a bowl, add mashed cod, cooked onion and garlic, beaten eggs and parsley, and stir together with a wooden spoon.

Season with salt and pepper to taste (you probably won't need salt, as there will be some from the cod). Shape mixture into small patties and refrigerate for at least 30 minutes until firm.

Heat about 1½-inches olive oil in a large heavy-based fry pan over medium heat until very hot. Add patties, a few at a time, and cook for 3–4 minutes, turning once, until golden brown.

Drain on paper towels and serve hot with lemon wedges and alioli.

Chickpeas & Chorizo

SERVES 4

7 ounces dried chickpeas
cold water, to soak and cook
   chickpeas
4 cloves
1 cinnamon stick
3 tablespoons olive oil
1 clove garlic, crushed
1 small onion, finely chopped

12 ounces cured chorizo
   sausage, cut into small cubes
2 tablespoons dry sherry
   (optional)
salt and freshly ground black
   pepper
$^1/_3$ cup chopped fresh flat-leaf
   parsley

Soak chickpeas in cold water overnight. Drain, then put in a saucepan and cover with fresh cold water. Add the cloves and cinnamon stick. Bring to a boil and simmer covered for 45 minutes or until tender. Add a little more water if needed during cooking. Drain.

Heat the olive oil in a large non-stick fry pan over medium heat. Add garlic and onion and sauté, stirring occasionally, until softened. Add chorizo and sauté for 2–3 minutes until lightly browned and heated through. Add drained chickpeas and sherry (if using), then stir for a few minutes until heated through. Season to taste. Sprinkle with chopped parsley and serve.

✖ You can substitute a 14-ounce can of chickpeas for dried chickpeas. If so, drain, rinse, add fresh water, cloves and cinnamon, and simmer for 5 minutes before adding to the pan.

Garlic & Chili Mushrooms

SERVES 4

2 tablespoons olive oil, plus
  extra to moisten
5 cloves garlic, crushed
9 ounces button mushrooms,
  stems trimmed
4 tablespoons dry sherry
2 tablespoons freshly squeezed
  lemon juice

1 small dried chili pepper,
  crushed
¼ teaspoon sweet or hot
  Spanish paprika
salt and freshly ground black
  pepper
½ cup finely chopped fresh
  flat-leaf parsley

Heat olive oil in a large, non-stick fry pan over medium heat. When hot, add garlic and sauté for about 1 minute (don't let it burn).

Add the mushrooms, sherry, lemon juice, chili pepper and paprika. Cook, stirring, for 4–5 minutes, until mushrooms soften. Add a little extra olive oil if the mixture seems too dry (but remember that the mushrooms will gradually release moisture).

Season with salt and pepper to taste and stir chopped parsley through. Serve warm or at room temperature.

Chorizo in Red Wine

SERVES 4–6

1 pound 5 ounces fresh
  chorizo sausage
2 cups light red wine (a Rioja
  or a pinot noir are good)
6–8 black peppercorns,
  roughly crushed

2 sprigs fresh rosemary
olive oil for frying
1 tablespoon finely chopped
  fresh flat-leaf parsley, to
  serve

Prick chorizo all over. Place in a bowl, pour wine over, and add peppercorns and rosemary. Cover, and marinate for 24 hours. Drain.

Lightly oil a barbecue grill or large non-stick fry pan, and preheat to medium. Cook chorizo over medium heat for 6–8 minutes, until the surface is crispy. Slice into thick diagonal chunks.

Arrange chorizo chunks on a platter, scatter with fresh parsley and serve immediately.

Fava Bean Omelette

SERVES 4

10½ ounces fresh broad beans, shelled
boiling and cold water, to cook and rinse beans
3 tablespoons olive oil
1 small onion, chopped
2 cloves garlic, chopped
6 eggs
salt and freshly ground black pepper
2½ ounces Swiss cheese, grated

Cook the beans in boiling water for 4–5 minutes, until soft. Drain, rinse under cold water and drain again. Remove the outer skins to reveal the bright-green seeds.

Heat 2 tablespoons of the olive oil in a non-stick fry pan. Add the onion and garlic and cook for 3–4 minutes, until onion is softened.

Beat eggs lightly with salt and pepper. Add cooked onion mixture, beans, and the cheese, and stir through.

Heat the remaining olive oil in fry pan over medium heat. Add egg mixture, lower heat and cook gently until set. Serve warm or at room temperature, cut into small pieces for tapas, or in wedges served with salad as a light meal.

※ Fava is another name for broad beans. You can use frozen beans for this recipe if fresh are not available, but dried beans are not suitable.

Jamon-wrapped Fish

SERVES 4–6

1 pound 2 ounces firm white
fish fillets (such as cod,
grouper or halibut)
1 tablespoon hot Spanish
paprika
12 slices jamon (or prosciutto),
sliced into wide strips

2 tablespoons extra-virgin
olive oil, plus extra to
drizzle
freshly ground black pepper
lemon wedges, to serve

Preheat broiler to high.

Cut fish into bite-sized pieces. Sprinkle a little paprika on each piece, then wrap in a strip of ham and secure with a toothpick.

Put fish bundles under the broiler for 8–10 minutes, turning once or twice, until the fish is cooked through. Transfer to a warmed platter, drizzle with olive oil, and season with black pepper. Serve immediately, with lemon wedges.

Catalan Bread with Tomato

Pa amb tomaquet

SERVES 4

4 slices firm, good-quality
   bread
2 cloves garlic,
   cut in half lengthwise
2 vine-ripened tomatoes,
   peeled and thickly sliced

extra-virgin olive oil,
   for drizzling
salt and freshly ground black
   pepper

Lightly toast the bread slices, or grill over a wood-fired barbecue for a smoky taste. Cut each slice in half and rub with garlic.

Mash one slice of tomato and spread a little on each of the toasted bread slices. Lay the remaining tomato slices on top, drizzle with olive oil, season with salt and pepper, and serve.

※ This is a very popular tapa, or a snack at any time. Use ripe, full-flavored tomatoes and top-quality olive oil. Catalans often add ham, cheese, anchovies or other toppings with the tomatoes.

Jamon Iberico with Asparagus

SERVES 4

12 asparagus spears,
   ends trimmed
boiling and ice water, to cook
   and stop cooking asparagus
5 ounces thinly sliced jamon
   Iberico (good-quality cured
   ham or prosciutto)

2 tablespoons olive oil
freshly ground black pepper
½ cup romesco sauce (page
   240)

Cook asparagus in boiling water for 3–4 minutes until just starting to soften but still bright green. Drain, then plunge asparagus into ice water to stop the cooking. Drain well. Pat dry, then wrap each spear in a piece of ham (leave the tips showing).

Heat the olive oil in a non-stick fry pan, and when hot add the ham-wrapped asparagus. Fry for 2–3 minutes until ham starts to crisp. Drain quickly on paper towels, season with pepper and serve immediately with romesco sauce for dipping.

✕ Jamon Iberico, considered the king of jamon, is eaten in the simplest way, either with fresh bread or, as here, with seasonal asparagus. If you cannot buy this ham, use jamon serrano or prosciutto instead.

Ham Croquettes
Croquetas de jamon

SERVES 6

3 tablespoons unsalted butter

3 tablespoons all-purpose flour

2 cups milk

3½ ounces jamon serrano (or prosciutto), chopped

½ teaspoon ground nutmeg

salt and freshly ground black pepper

all-purpose flour, for dusting

2 eggs, lightly beaten

1 cup dried breadcrumbs

oil for deep-frying

Heat the butter in a heavy-based saucepan over medium heat, then stir in the flour and cook for 1 minute, stirring. Gradually add the milk and continue stirring for a few minutes, until the mixture forms a thick sauce. Remove from heat.

Stir ham and nutmeg into the sauce. Check seasoning and add salt and pepper to taste. Let cool.

Pour croquette mixture Into a baking dish. Cover and refrigerate for 2–3 hours, or overnight, until mixture is set. ❯

Use a spoon to scoop out small amounts of mixture, then shape into egg-shaped croquettes. Coat each croquette lightly in flour. Then dip into beaten egg, and lastly the breadcrumbs. Place croquettes on a tray and refrigerate for at least 30 minutes.

Heat about 2 inches of olive oil in a heavy-based saucepan over medium–high heat. Deep-fry croquettes in small batches until golden on all sides. Remove with a slotted spoon and drain on paper towels. Keep warm until all the croquettes are cooked.

Serve immediately.

※ If you have time, make the mixture the day before assembling the croquettes as it will be easier to handle.

Eggs with Tuna

Huevos con atun

MAKES 16

8 hard-boiled eggs, shelled
1 (3 1/2-ounce) can tuna in
   water or springwater,
   drained and mashed
4 tablespoons good-quality
   mayonnaise
2 tablespoons Dijon mustard

1 tablespoon freshly squeezed
   lemon juice
½ teaspoon sweet Spanish
   paprika, plus extra to serve
salt, to taste
finely chopped fresh flat-leaf
   parsley, for garnish

Halve the eggs lengthwise and scoop out yolks. Set whites aside. Mash yolks with the tuna, then add the mayonnaise, mustard, lemon juice, paprika and salt, mixing well.

Pile the tuna mixture into the egg-white halves. Cover and refrigerate until ready to serve.

To serve, sprinkle with parsley and dust with a little extra paprika if desired.

Kidneys with Sherry
Rinones al Jerez

SERVES 4

2 veal kidneys
water, to cover kidneys
2 tablespoons sherry vinegar
2 tablespoons olive oil
1 clove garlic, crushed
1 teaspoon hot or sweet
   Spanish paprika
1 sprig fresh thyme

1 tablespoon chopped fresh
   flat-leaf parsley
½ cup dry sherry
½ cup veal stock
salt and freshly ground black
   pepper
1 tablespoon fresh
   breadcrumbs

Skin kidneys and cut out the core, then slice thinly. Place in a ceramic or glass dish, cover with ¼ cup water and the sherry vinegar, and let soak for 30 minutes. Drain well and pat dry with paper towels.

Heat the olive oil in a heavy-based pan over medium heat, add garlic and sauté for 1 minute until just soft. Add kidney slices and cook for 2–3 minutes, turning once, until seared. Add paprika, thyme and parsley, then pour in the sherry and cook for 1 minute. Add veal stock to pan, season with salt and pepper, and cover. Reduce heat and simmer for 15–20 minutes, checking occasionally, until kidneys are soft. Gently stir in the breadcrumbs until sauce thickens a little. Check seasoning and serve hot.

Padron Peppers

SERVES 4

1 pound 2 ounces padron
   peppers
2–3 tablespoons olive oil
salt flakes (delicate finishing
   salt)

Wash peppers and pat dry. Leave whole, with stems attached (to hold when eating).

Heat the olive oil in a heavy-based fry pan and when hot, toss in the peppers and sauté, turning so that they are coated in the olive oil. Cook for a few minutes, turning until peppers are lightly blistered and starting to soften.

Transfer to a warmed serving plate, sprinkle generously with salt flakes and serve immediately.

✕ Padron peppers are small green chili peppers that are usually – but not always – mild. About one in every ten is extremely hot, so beware!

Fried Black Pudding
Morcilla frita

MAKES 10

1 tablespoon olive oil
1 clove garlic, sliced
1 red onion, finely chopped
1 teaspoon sweet Spanish
   paprika
1 sprig fresh oregano
9 ounces black pudding (blood
   sausage or morcilla), cut
   into 10 slices

10 slices bread from baguette,
   cut on an angle
2 tablespoons dry sherry
salt and freshly ground black
   pepper

Heat the olive oil in a large fry pan over medium heat, then add the garlic, onion, paprika and oregano, and sauté for 3–4 minutes, until onion is softened.

Add black pudding and cook for about 4 minutes, turning once or twice, until lightly browned. Put a piece of black pudding on each slice of bread and arrange on a serving plate.

Add sherry to pan, season with salt and pepper, and heat through. Drizzle a little of the sauce over the black pudding and serve immediately.

✕ Boudin rouge or blutwurst can replace morcilla.

Paprika-spiced Almonds

SERVES 6

2 tablespoons extra-virgin
   olive oil
1 pound 2 ounces blanched
   almonds
1 teaspoon hot Spanish
   paprika
1 teaspoon ground cumin
1 tablespoon salt flakes
   (delicate finishing salt)

Heat the olive oil in a fry pan over medium heat. Add almonds and cook, stirring, for about 5 minutes or until they are golden brown.

Add paprika and cumin to pan and stir to coat almonds. Remove from the heat and add salt flakes. Serve warm or cold.

Piquillos with Anchovies

SERVES 4–6

10–12 anchovy fillets in oil,
　　drained
8 ounces pickled piquillo
　　peppers, sliced
extra-virgin olive oil for
　　drizzling
2 tablespoons finely chopped
　　fresh flat-leaf parsley
crusty bread or toast triangles,
　　to serve

If anchovy fillets are long, cut them in half.

Arrange pepper slices on a platter, then lay anchovy fillets on top. Drizzle a little olive oil over the dish and sprinkle with chopped parsley.

Serve at room temperature, with crusty bread or toast.

✖ Piquillo peppers are a variety of red chili pepper, which are sweet rather than hot. Roasted, peeled and pickled, they are available in jars and cans from specialty food stores.

Pork Skewers
Pinchitos

SERVES 4

cold water, to soak bamboo skewers
3 cloves garlic, chopped
1 teaspoon sea salt
½ teaspoon each of hot Spanish paprika, coriander, cumin, turmeric, cardamom and fenugreek
pinch of saffron threads
freshly ground black pepper
1 tablespoon freshly squeezed lemon juice
3 tablespoons olive oil
1 pound 2 ounces lean pork (such as tenderloin or top loin), cut into small cubes
lemon wedges, to serve

Soak 4-6 bamboo skewers in cold water for at least 1 hour.

Crush garlic and salt in a mortar, then add spices, lemon juice and olive oil, and grind to a paste.

Thread pork onto skewers. Place skewers in a shallow dish and coat with the spice paste. Cover and refrigerate for 2–3 hours.

Preheat grill or barbecue to high. Grill skewers for about 4 minutes, turning once or twice, until cooked.

Transfer to a warmed plate and serve with lemon wedges on the side.

※ These small, spicy pork kebabs reflect Moorish influences. Pinchito spice mix is available in some specialty food stores: this recipe includes many of the spices in the traditional blend.

Pork Rolls with Jamon Serrano

SERVES 8

8 boneless pork cutlets, about
  ½ inch thick
freshly ground black pepper
8 thin slices jamon serrano (or
  prosciutto)
2 eggs

2 tablespoons milk
1 cup dry breadcrumbs
oil for frying
alioli (page 238) or
  mayonnaise, to serve

Pound cutlets with a rolling pin or mallet until flattened and about twice their original diameter. Season with pepper, then lay a slice of ham on each cutlet. Roll up tightly (secure with a toothpick if necessary).

Lightly whisk eggs and milk. Dip each cutlet into the egg mixture, then into the breadcrumbs, pressing to make sure rolls are well coated.

Heat oil to a depth of about ¾ inch in a heavy-based fry pan over medium heat. When hot, but not smoking, add rolls in batches and fry for about 5–6 minutes, turning carefully to make sure they are golden and crisp on all sides. Remove from pan and drain on paper towels. Keep warm until all rolls are cooked.

Cut rolls in thick slices on an angle and serve hot or warm, with alioli or mayonnaise on the side.

✕ Jamon serrano is dry-cured "mountain ham".

Fried Cheese
Queso frito

MAKES ABOUT 20

8 ½ ounces manchego cheese (or use provolone or mozzarella)
all-purpose flour, for dusting
2 eggs, lightly beaten
1 cup dry breadcrumbs
salt and freshly ground black pepper
olive oil for deep-frying
1 tablespoon chopped fresh dill, and lemon wedges, to serve

Cut cheese into sticks about ⅜-inch thick and 2-inches long. Dust lightly with flour, dip into beaten eggs and then into the breadcrumbs. Place cheese sticks on a plate, cover and refrigerate for at least 1 hour until coating is firm.

Pour about 2 inches olive oil into a heavy-based saucepan and place over medium heat until hot. Fry cheese sticks a few at a time. Remove with slotted spoon and drain on paper towels. Keep warm until all are cooked.

Serve immediately, sprinkled with fresh dill, with lemon wedges on the side.

✕ To ensure the cheese sticks are crisp on the outside and soft inside, keep the olive oil hot at 350°F but do not let it start smoking. If the olive oil gets too hot, remove from the heat for a minute or two.

Quince & Blue Cheese Montaditos

MAKES 12

12 thick slices good-quality
    bread from baguette, cut on
    an angle
2 tablespoons extra-virgin
    olive oil
3 cloves garlic, halved

4 ounces quince paste
4 ounces soft blue-vein cheese
    (such as Gorgonzola or
    Roquefort at room
    temperature)

Preheat oven to 350°F.

Brush both sides of the bread slices with olive oil and rub with garlic. Place on baking sheet in preheated oven and cook for 5 minutes, turning once, until toasted and golden. Remove from oven and allow to cool.

Place a slice of quince paste on each bread slice. Top with blue cheese and serve.

※ A montadito is similar to Italian bruschetta – basically a slice of toasted bread with a savory topping.

※ Quince paste is a jam or marmalade made from quince, an aromatic fruit that's high in pectin and must be cooked.

Spiced Olives

MAKES ABOUT 2 CUPS

1 teaspoon fennel seeds
1 tablespoon cumin seeds
1 tablespoon coriander seeds
⅓ cup olive oil
3 cloves garlic, finely sliced
1 tablespoon dried chili flakes

1 tablespoon finely grated
  lemon zest
1 pound 2 ounces mixed olives
  (black and green)
½ cup finely chopped fresh
  flat-leaf parsley

Place fennel, cumin and coriander seeds in a fry pan over medium heat and toast until lightly browned and fragrant.

Heat olive oil in a small pan until just warm. Add garlic, chili flakes, toasted seeds and lemon zest, and stir over medium heat for 2–3 minutes, to infuse olive oil.

Place olives in a bowl, pour warmed olive oil mixture over and stir to coat. Cover with food wrap and let marinate at room temperature at least a few hours before serving. Stir occasionally.

Stir chopped parsley through before serving.

✖ To keep the olives for 3–4 weeks, store in a clean, sterilized jar in the refrigerator. Use a clean spoon when removing olives from the jar.

Anchovy & Olive Sticks
Gildas

MAKES 10

20 pitted green olives
10 pickled piquillo peppers,
    cut into strips
10 anchovies in oil, drained

Thread an olive, a strip of pepper and a folded anchovy onto a toothpick, then finish with another green olive. Repeat with remaining ingredients. Arrange on a plate and serve.

✕ These small, salty morsels are a favorite at tapas bars. The word *gilda* means lollipop.

Spinach Empanadas

SERVES 4

3 tablespoons olive oil
3 cloves garlic, crushed
9 ounces vine-ripened
   tomatoes, chopped
pinch of Spanish paprika
1 pound 10 ounces spinach,
   rinsed and chopped
½ cup pine nuts, lightly toasted

2 hard-boiled eggs, shelled
   and chopped
salt and freshly ground black
   pepper
2 sheets pre-rolled, ready-to-
   bake short-crust pastry
1 egg, lightly beaten

Heat olive oil in a fry pan. Add garlic and sauté for 1–2 minutes until soft. Add tomatoes and paprika, and cook for 10–15 minutes over low heat, stirring occasionally, until mixture thickens into a sauce. Add spinach and pine nuts, stir through and cook until spinach is wilted. The mixture should be fairly dry; if not, cook over high heat to reduce. Stir chopped egg through mixture and season to taste.

Preheat oven to 350°F. Line two baking sheets with parchment (baking) paper. Cut pastry into 5-inch rounds. Spoon a little filling into center of each pastry, then fold over and pinch to seal edges. Brush lightly with beaten egg and bake for 15–20 minutes, until golden brown. Serve hot or at room temperature.

Fried Spanish Olives

1½ ounces soft goat cheese

9 ounces large, pitted green
Spanish olives, drained

¾ cup fresh breadcrumbs

½ cup finely grated Parmesan
cheese

¼ teaspoon hot Spanish
paprika

1 egg, beaten with 1 tablespoon
water

⅓ cup cup all-purpose flour

olive oil for deep-frying

bread cube, for testing oil

Line a baking sheet or flat plate with parchment (baking) paper. Stuff a little of the goat's cheese into each olive, using a small spoon.

Mix together breadcrumbs, Parmesan cheese and paprika. Dip olives in flour to dust lightly, then into the beaten egg and, finally, the breadcrumbs. Place on prepared baking sheet or plate. When all the olives are crumbed, refrigerate for 15–30 minutes.

Heat about 1½ inches olive oil in a heavy-based saucepan over medium–high heat. To test, drop in a small cube of bread – it should sizzle and turn brown within a few seconds. Fry olives in batches until golden, then remove with a slotted spoon and drain on paper towels. Repeat with the remaining olives.

Serve immediately.

Cheese & Fig Open Sandwich
Montaditos de manchego

SERVES 8

16 thick slices bread from
    baguette, cut on an angle
4 ounces butter, softened
2 tablespoons fig jam
8 slices ham

4 ounces manchego cheese,
    pared into thin slices
extra-virgin olive oil, to serve
freshly ground black pepper

Preheat the oven to 300°F. Place bread slices on a baking sheet, place in the oven and bake for 8–10 minutes, turning once, until golden on both sides.

Mix butter and fig jam, and spread on the prepared toasted bread slices. Top with ham and cheese slices. Drizzle with a little olive oil, season with black pepper, and serve.

✕ If manchego is not available, you could use another semi-hard cheese such as gruyère.

Olive, Anchovy & Caper Puffs

SERVES 4

1 tablespoon baby capers,
    rinsed
4 canned anchovy fillets in oil,
    drained and chopped
3 tablespoons Spanish
    tapenade (page 242)

2 tablespoons finely chopped
    fresh flat-leaf parsley
2 sheets pre-rolled, ready-to-
    bake puff pastry

Preheat the oven to 400°F. Line two baking sheets with parchment (baking) paper.

Put capers, anchovies, tapenade and parsley in a small bowl and mix well. Spread half the mixture onto one sheet of pastry, roll up pastry firmly to form a log, pressing well to seal the edge. Using a sharp knife, cut into ¾-inch slices and place flat on prepared baking sheets.

Repeat with remaining mixture and the other pastry sheet.

Place pastries in preheated oven and bake for 5–6 minutes, until puffed and golden. Transfer to a warmed serving plate and serve.

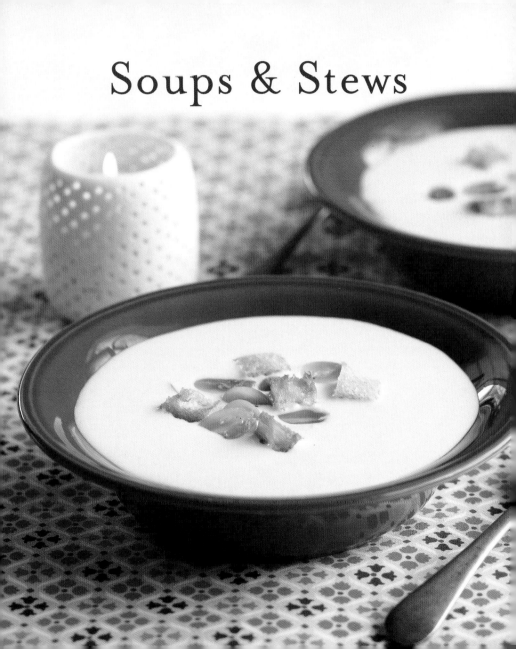

Soups & Stews

Spain's most famous soup is undoubtedly gazpacho; a chilled, tomato-based mixture. It comes in numerous regional guises, some smooth, some chunky, but all refreshing in the country's often searingly hot summers. A less familiar, delicate version is the 'white' gazpacho — the almond-based ajo blanco, typically garnished with cool green grapes and crisp croutons.

Other traditional soups and stews are much more substantial — rich broths laden with seafood, or sustaining peasant fare; hearty with meat, vegetables, and, of course, flavored with smoky Spanish paprika.

< ALMOND GAZPACHO (PAGE 62)

Almond Gazpacho
Ajo blanco

SERVES 4–6

6 slices firm, stale white bread, crusts removed
cold water, to soak bread
2 cloves garlic, crushed
1 teaspoon salt flakes (delicate finishing salt)
3½ ounces blanched almonds
½ cup extra-virgin olive oil
¼ cup dry sherry
1½ cups vegetable stock
ice water, to thin soup
1 cup seedless green grapes, washed, stems removed
1 cup croutons (see note next page)

Soak bread in a small amount of cold water until soft, then squeeze out excess moisture.

Pound garlic and salt flakes in a mortar to form a paste. Blend paste with almonds in a food processor or blender until almonds are finely ground. Add the soaked bread and process again, then pour in olive oil in a thin steady stream until mixture thickens. Add sherry and stock and continue to blend. The soup should be smooth.

Cover and refrigerate for 2–3 hours.

Check seasoning before serving – it may need extra salt flakes. If soup is too thick, add a little ice water.

Pour into individual bowls, scatter with grapes (cut them in half if they are large) and croutons, and serve.

✕ Bread is often used to thicken Spanish soups, either soaked and pounded to a paste, or added as crumbs or in pieces and stirred through. To make croutons, cut stale crusty bread into small cubes. Fry in hot oil for about 2 minutes, or until golden and crisp, then drain on paper towels.

Chickpea & Cod Soup

SERVES 6

5 tablespoons olive oil
1 onion, chopped
1 pound 2 ounces chickpeas,
    soaked overnight, drained
water, to cover chickpeas
1 bay leaf
9 ounces salt cod, soaked (see
    page 4), cut into bite-sized
    pieces
9 ounces potatoes, peeled and
    finely chopped

2 cloves garlic, chopped
1 tablespoon finely chopped
    fresh flat-leaf parsley
½ teaspoon ground cumin
½ teaspoon mild Spanish
    paprika
1 bunch spinach, leaves rinsed
    and chopped
salt and freshly ground black
    pepper

Heat 2 tablespoons of the olive oil in a heavy-based saucepan until hot, then sauté onion for 3–4 minutes, stirring occasionally, until it is transparent. Add chickpeas and bay leaf, pour in 1¼ quarts water and bring to a boil. Cover pan, reduce heat and simmer for about 45 minutes, removing any scum from the surface, until chickpeas are starting to soften.

Add cod and cook for another 30 minutes. Add potatoes and cook for an additional 15 minutes, until vegetables and chickpeas are soft.

Pound remaining olive oil, garlic, parsley, cumin and paprika in a mortar to form a rough paste.

Stir chopped spinach into soup and heat through. Check for seasoning, adding salt and pepper to taste.

To serve, ladle soup into warmed bowls and top each with a scoop of the parsley paste.

※ You will need to start this recipe a day ahead, to allow for soaking the chickpeas and the salted cod.

Galician Fish Soup

SERVES 4

3 pound 5 ounces fresh mixed
  seafood (see note page 68),
  cleaned
1/3 cup olive oil
2 onions, thinly sliced
1 clove garlic, crushed
2 tablespoons chopped fresh
  flat-leaf parsley
1 tablespoon sweet Spanish
  paprika
1 small fresh red chili pepper,
  sliced, seeds removed

salt
water, to cover seafood
1/2 cup cup dry wine (such as
  Chardonnay or Sauvignon
  Blanc)
freshly ground black pepper

CROUTONS

2 slices day-old sourdough
  bread, lightly toasted
extra-virgin olive oil

Pat seafood dry, then slice into generous, bite-sized pieces. Remove shells from crustaceans. Place seafood in a large saucepan or stockpot, with the olive oil, onion, garlic, half the parsley, the paprika and the red chili pepper. Sprinkle with salt, cover and leave for 30 minutes.

Add enough water to the pan to cover the seafood completely. Bring to a boil, then add the wine, cover and simmer for 15 20 minutes. **>**

To make the croutons, cut toasted bread slices into 4 triangles and brush with olive oil.

Check soup for seasoning and add pepper if needed. Put a crouton in the bottom of each serving bowl, place a few pieces of seafood on top and ladle the broth over at once. Sprinkle with the remaining chopped parsley and serve.

✕ For this stew-like soup, choose fish such as cod, grouper, orange roughy or sole, shellfish such as crab or prawns, and baby squid. If using mussels, scrub shells and add them to the soup in the last 5 minutes of cooking. Discard any mussels if the shells do not open.

Garlic Soup

SERVES 6

5 tablespoons olive oil, plus
    extra for sautéing bread
6 cloves garlic, peeled
12 thin slices firm bread from
    baguette, crusts removed
6 eggs
1 teaspoon Spanish paprika

1⅔ quarts chicken or vegetable
    stock
salt and freshly ground black
    pepper
2 tablespoons finely chopped
    fresh flat-leaf parsley

Preheat oven to 350°F. Place 6 ovenproof bowls on a baking sheet.

Heat olive oil in a large, non-stick saucepan over medium heat. Add garlic and sauté for a few minutes. Remove garlic from pan and set aside.

Add slices of bread to pan in batches, and sauté until golden on both sides (add a little extra oil if needed). Put a piece of fried bread in the bottom of each soup bowl. Break an egg onto each slice.

Return garlic to the pan, add paprika and stock, season with salt and pepper and bring to a boil, then ladle broth over carefully.

Place baking sheet with soup bowls in preheated oven and cook for about 5 minutes, until the eggwhite is set but the yolk is still runny. Remove from oven, sprinkle with parsley and serve.

Spanish Tomato Soup with Goat Cheese Toasts

SERVES 6

¹/₃ cup olive oil

1 red onion, chopped

2 cloves garlic, sliced

1 red bell pepper, deseeded and chopped

4 pounds 6 ounces vine-ripened tomatoes, peeled and chopped

1 teaspoon sweet Spanish paprika

1 teaspoon ground cumin

salt and freshly ground black pepper

6 thin slices of bread from baguette, lightly toasted

2 ounces soft goat cheese

Heat about 3 tablespoons of the olive oil in a large, heavy-based saucepan over low heat. Add onion, garlic and red bell pepper, and cook, stirring occasionally, for about 10 minutes until vegetables are quite soft.

Add tomatoes, paprika and cumin, cover pan and simmer for 20 minutes. Allow soup to cool a little, then blend in batches in a food processor or blender until smooth.

Return soup to heat, season with salt and pepper, and reheat.

Brush toasted bread slices with olive oil, then spread with goat cheese. Pour soup into warmed bowls, top each with a prepared bread slice and serve immediately.

Lentil & Pork Soup

SERVES 4–6

3 tablespoons olive oil

2 cloves garlic, crushed

2 stalks celery, thickly sliced

2 medium-sized carrots, thickly sliced

2 boneless pork loin chops, cut into cubes

4 medium-sized potatoes, peeled and cut into small cubes

1 pound 2 ounces dried brown lentils, rinsed

½ teaspoon ground cumin

water, to cover meat and vegetables

salt and freshly ground black pepper

Heat olive oil in a large, heavy-based, non-stick saucepan over medium heat. Add garlic and sauté for 1 minute. Add celery and carrots, sauté again for a few minutes, then add cubed pork and sauté for a few minutes more, until meat is lightly browned all over.

Add potatoes, lentils and cumin, then add enough water to cover meat and vegetables. Bring to a boil, cover, reduce heat and simmer for 40–50 minutes. Stir occasionally, and add a little extra water if needed. When soup is quite thick and lentils are soft, season with salt and pepper. Serve hot with crusty bread.

✖ Lentils and other legumes frequently feature in Spanish soups and stews. If you prefer, you can leave out the pork – this still makes a substantial dish.

Gazpacho Andalucia

SERVE 4–6

2 cloves garlic, crushed
1 teaspoon salt
1 slice firm, day-old bread,
    crusts removed
water, to soak bread
1 pound 10 ounces vine-ripened
    tomatoes, roughly chopped
2 English (seedless)
    cucumbers, chopped
1 green bell pepper, deseeded
    and roughly chopped

2 tablespoons red-wine vinegar
$^1/_3$ cup extra-virgin olive oil
salt and freshly ground black
    pepper
1 cup croutons
    (see note page 63), to serve
extra cucumber, deseeded and
    finely chopped, to serve
2 hard-boiled eggs, shelled
    and chopped, to serve

Pound garlic and salt in a mortar until it forms a paste. Soak bread in water until softened, then squeeze to remove excess moisture.

Put garlic paste, soaked bread, tomatoes, cucumber, green bell pepper and vinegar in food processor or blender and process until blended to your preferred texture (from smooth to chunky). Pour olive oil in slowly and continue blending. Season with pepper and extra salt if needed.

Cover and refrigerate for 2–3 hours until well chilled. Serve with small bowls of croutons, cucumber and hard-boiled eggs on the side.

Rustic Squid Stew

SERVES 4

3 tablespoons olive oil
1 pound 10 ounces squid,
   cleaned and cut into rings
   (leave tentacles in one piece
   if not too long)
1 red onion, finely chopped
2 cloves garlic, crushed
14 ounces canned chopped
   tomatoes
1 small fresh chili pepper,
   deseeded and sliced

1¾ cups fish stock
1 teaspoon sweet Spanish
   paprika
1 bay leaf
salt and freshly ground black
   pepper
2 tablespoons finely chopped
   fresh flat-leaf parsley, to
   serve

Heat olive oil in a large, heavy-based pan over high heat. Add squid and cook, stirring occasionally, until golden brown.

Add onion and garlic and cook for 6–7 minutes, stirring occasionally, until transparent and starting to caramelize. Add tomatoes, red chili pepper, stock, paprika and bay leaf and bring to a boil. Cover, reduce heat to very low and simmer for 2 hours. Remove the bay leaf, check for seasoning and add salt and pepper if needed. Spoon into warmed bowls, scatter with parsley and serve.

✕ For squid to be tender, it must be cooked very quickly or very slowly. This slow-simmer method results in a melt-in-the-mouth texture.

White Bean & Sausage Stew

Fabada Asturiana

SERVES 6–8

2 pound dried broad beans, or cannellini beans, soaked overnight
2 pounds fresh chorizo sausage
1 pound salt pork or ham hock
6 cloves garlic, halved
6 peppercorns, roughly crushed
1 teaspoon sweet Spanish paprika

12 ounces fresh chorizo, whole
12 ounces black pudding (morcilla), whole
cold water, to cover bean and sausage mixture
salt, to taste
finely chopped fresh flat-leaf parsley

Drain beans and put in a large, heavy-based saucepan. Add pork, garlic, peppercorns, paprika, chorizo and black pudding. Fill with cold water to cover by about 1 inch. Bring to a boil over medium heat, then reduce heat, cover and cook for about 1 hour. Check occasionally, stirring gently. Add more water, if necessary, to keep ingredients covered. After 1 hour, add salt to taste and continue simmering until beans are soft. (Don't boil, or beans may split and lose their skins.)

Remove from heat and leave for 5–10 minutes. Remove pork and sausages from the pan and slice thickly. Arrange meats in warmed bowls, then spoon beans onto plates and ladle on some of the broth. Scatter with chopped parsley and serve.

✖ Fabada Asturiana is similar to French cassoulet. Traditionally, the meat is served separately from the broth and beans, but you can serve together in bowls if you wish.

Gypsy Stew
Olla Gitana

SERVES 6

1 pound 12 ounces canned chickpeas, rinsed and drained

9 ounces green beans, trimmed and cut into 2-inch lengths

14 ounces fresh pumpkin, peeled and chopped

2 ¼ quarts good-quality chicken or vegetable stock

small bunch spinach, washed and chopped

salt and freshly ground black pepper

about 3 tablespoons olive oil

2 cloves garlic, chopped

12 blanched almonds, chopped

1 piece stale, firm white bread, crusts removed, cut into cubes

2 medium-sized, vine-ripened tomatoes, peeled and chopped

2 pears, barely ripe, peeled and cut into small cubes

1 teaspoon sweet Spanish paprika

1 tablespoon sherry vinegar

a few threads saffron, crumbled, and then soaked in a little warm water

Put chickpeas, beans and pumpkin in a large, heavy-based saucepan, add the stock, bring to a boil and simmer, uncovered, for about 10–15 minutes until vegetables are cooked. >

Stir chopped spinach into pan and season to taste with salt and pepper.

Heat two-thirds of the olive oil in a fry pan over medium heat. Add garlic, almonds and bread and cook for a few minutes until almonds are toasted and the bread lightly fried. Pound to a thick paste in a mortar, or blend in a food processor or blender.

Wipe fry pan with paper towels, and add remaining olive oil. Add tomatoes, pears, paprika and vinegar, and cook over medium heat, stirring occasionally, for about 10 minutes.

Add the bread and almond paste, saffron (and soaking liquid) and cooked tomato mixture to the chickpeas and vegetables. Simmer for a few minutes for flavors to combine and adjust seasoning if needed.

Serve hot, with plenty of fresh bread.

Rabbit & Tomato Stew

SERVES 4

3 tablespoons olive oil, plus
  more for sautéing
1 (4 pound 6-ounce) rabbit,
  cut into 8–10 pieces (ask
  your butcher to do this)
2 cloves garlic, sliced
1 brown-skinned onion, finely
  chopped
14 ounces canned crushed
  tomatoes

2 stalks celery, finely chopped
2 bay leaves, fresh if possible
1 sprig fresh thyme
1 sprig fresh tarragon
1 cup dry white wine
salt and freshly ground black
  pepper

Heat olive oil in a large, heavy-based non-stick fry pan over medium–high heat. When hot, add rabbit pieces and sauté until lightly browned all over. Remove rabbit from pan and set aside.

Add a little extra olive oil to the pan if necessary. Add garlic and onion, sauté for 2–3 minutes, then add tomatoes, celery, bay leaves, thyme, tarragon and wine, and stir to combine. Put rabbit pieces back into the sauce, bring to a boil and cook over high heat until liquid reduces by about one-third.

Reduce heat, cover and simmer over very low heat for 1½–2 hours, until meat is very tender and pulls easily away from the bone. Check seasoning. Serve hot, with crusty bread to soak up the sauce.

Basque Fish Stew
Marmitako

SERVES 4

3 tablespoons olive oil
2 cloves garlic, chopped
1 red onion, thinly sliced
1 pound 2 ounces potatoes, peeled and cubed
14 ounces canned crushed tomatoes
2 teaspoons Spanish paprika
¾ cup fish stock
1 bay leaf

14 ounces canned chickpeas, rinsed and drained
1 pound 5 ounces skinless tuna or cod fillets, cut into large portions
salt and freshly ground black pepper
1 tablespoon finely grated lemon zest
2 tablespoons finely chopped fresh flat-leaf parsley

Heat olive oil in a heavy-based saucepan over medium heat. Add garlic and onion and sauté for 4–5 minutes, until softened and starting to caramelize. Add potatoes, tomatoes, paprika, stock and bay leaf. Cover and simmer for 15 minutes, until potatoes are cooked.

Add chickpeas and stir. Then add fish, bring to simmering, reduce heat, cover and simmer for 10–12 minutes, until fish is cooked through. Remove bay leaf, check seasoning and add salt and pepper to taste.

Mix lemon zest and parsley together, sprinkle over stew and serve immediately.

※ Marmitako means "from the pot".

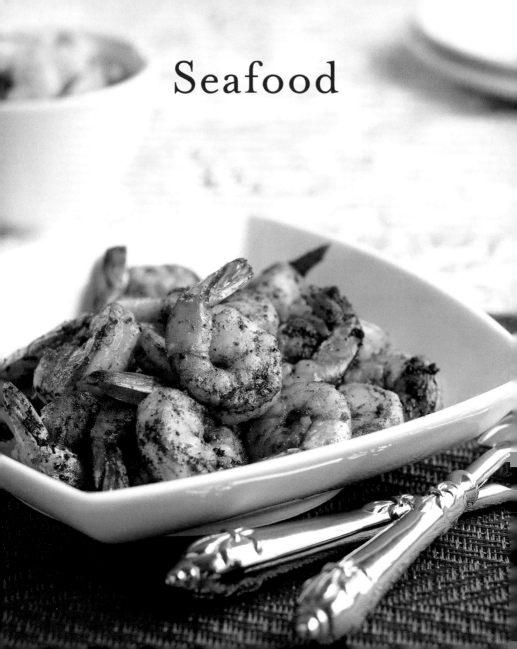

Seafood

Spain's lengthy coastline provides an abundance of seafood. A fresh, local catch is often simply grilled or pan-fried, especially when served as tapas. That said, you will also find seafood poached in wine, or battered and golden-fried, in fragrant soups and stews, pickled and cured; salt cod (*bacalao*) is ubiquitous and served in a myriad of ways.

You will also find seafood recipes in the Tapas and Soups & Stews sections.

< PAPRIKA PRAWNS WITH AVOCADO SALSA (PAGE 86)

Paprika Prawns
with Avocado Salsa

6 tablespoons butter, melted

3 tablespoons olive oil

1 teaspoon salt

freshly ground black pepper

1 tablespoon sweet Spanish
paprika

2 teaspoons ground cumin

2 pounds 3 ounces raw (green)
prawns

AVOCADO SALSA

1 small red onion, halved and
thinly sliced

2 cloves garlic, sliced

1 avocado, peeled, pit removed
and cubed

2 tablespoons extra-virgin
olive oil

juice of 1 lemon

1 tablespoon sweet Spanish
paprika

Place butter, olive oil, salt, pepper, paprika and cumin in a large bowl and mix well. Shell and devein the prawns, leaving tails intact. Add prawns to the bowl, stir to coat and then set aside.

To make the avocado salsa, put onion, garlic and avocado in a small bowl. Whisk olive oil, lemon juice and paprika together, pour over the avocado and stir gently to coat. Cover and refrigerate while prawns are cooking.

Preheat the oven broiler or barbecue to hot. Cook prawns for 4–5 minutes, turning once or twice and brushing with marinade, until flesh turns pink and opaque. Serve immediately with avocado salsa.

Garlic Prawns
Gambas al ajillo

SERVES 4

9 ounces small raw (green)
   prawns
3 tablespoons olive oil
2 cloves garlic, finely sliced
2 small dried chili peppers,
   crushed
salt
bread, to soak up juices

Shell and devein the prawns, leaving the tails intact. Pat dry with paper towels.

Heat the olive oil in a medium-sized non-stick fry pan, or one or more *cazuelas* (see page 9). Add garlic, chili peppers and prawns and cook over medium–high heat for about 3 minutes, until prawns are opaque and garlic and chili peppers are crisp. Sprinkle with salt and serve immediately, with bread to soak up any juices.

✖ If you prefer to cook the prawns in a pan, transfer them to a warmed *cazuela* to serve.

Mussels in White Wine

SERVES 4

¼ cup olive oil

1 onion, finely chopped

2 cloves garlic, chopped

2 large, vine-ripened
tomatoes, peeled and
chopped

2 cups dry white wine

3 pounds 5 ounces mussels,
scrubbed and debearded

2 ounces unsalted butter

4 tablespoons freshly ground
black pepper

2 tablespoons finely sliced
spring onions (optional)

bread, to serve

Heat the olive oil in a large, deep saucepan over medium heat. Add onion and garlic and sauté for 3–4 minutes, then add the tomatoes and cook for an additional 5–6 minutes, until softened.

Add the white wine to the pan, bring to a boil, then add the mussels. Reduce heat, cover, and steam for 5–6 minutes, shaking the pan a little, until mussels have opened. Discard any mussels that do not open.

Transfer cooked mussels with a slotted spoon to a warmed bowl. Strain the cooking liquid, then return it to the pan. Add butter and pepper, bring to a boil, stir in spring onions (if using) and simmer for 1 minute. Spoon sauce over the mussels and serve with plenty of good bread.

Baby Squid on the Grill
Calamares a la plancha

SERVES 4

1 pound 2 ounces baby squid
  tubes
2 tablespoons olive oil, plus
  extra for grilling
3 tablespoons freshly squeezed
  lemon juice
grated zest of 1 lemon
2 cloves garlic, crushed

$^{1}/_{3}$ cup finely chopped fresh
  flat-leaf parsley, plus extra
  to serve
salt and freshly ground pepper
lemon wedges, to serve
  (optional)

Cut the squid tubes open, rinse, and pat dry. Slice into large pieces.

Put olive oil, lemon juice, lemon zest, garlic and parsley in a non-metal bowl
and mix. Add squid, season with salt and pepper and stir to coat. Cover with
food wrap and refrigerate for at least 30 minutes.

Preheat grill to high, or brush a griddle pan with olive oil and place over high
heat. Add squid pieces and cook for 1–2 minutes, turning once, until just
cooked. Serve immediately, with extra parsley and lemon if desired.

✕ It is important to cook the squid very quickly, or it will become tough. This form of cooking,
traditionally on a very hot metal plate (*plancha*), is used in Spanish cuisine for many types
of seafood, as well as meats.

Galician-style Octopus
Pulpo Gallego

SERVES 4

tentacles from 2 octopus, about 2¼ pounds, cleaned

cold water, to cover and rinse octopus

2 cloves garlic, sliced

½ onion

6 peppercorns, roughly crushed

1 bay leaf

1 teaspoon salt

½ cup freshly squeezed lemon juice

6 tablespoons extra-virgin olive oil

salt and freshly ground black pepper

Put octopus tentacles in a large saucepan, cover with cold water, and add garlic, onion, peppercorns, bay leaf, salt and half the lemon juice. Bring to a boil, then reduce heat, cover and simmer for 45–60 minutes, or until tender.

Drain and rinse under cold water. Cut away any dark skin, then slice into bite-sized pieces.

Whisk remaining lemon juice with the olive oil and season with salt and pepper. Pour this dressing over the octopus and let marinate for at least two hours before serving. Serve at room temperature.

✕ This semi-pickled octopus will keep, covered, in the refrigerator for up to 1 week.

Whitebait with Saffron Alioli

SERVES 4

a few saffron threads,
    crumbled
warm water, to soak saffron
1 cup alioli (page 238)
14 ounces whitebait,
    patted dry

cornstarch for dusting
olive oil for deep-frying
salt

Soak saffron in a little warm water for 10 minutes. Mix this liquid with the alioli, cover and refrigerate for 1–2 hours to allow flavor to develop.

Dip whitebait into cornstarch and shake off any excess.

Pour about 2 inches olive oil into a large, heavy-based saucepan over medium–high heat. When the olive oil is hot, cook whitebait in small batches until golden and crisp (about 5 minutes). Remove with a slotted spoon, drain on paper towels, season with a little salt and serve immediately with the saffron alioli.

✳ Whitebait are little fish, such as herring, sardines or smelt.

Sardines Chargrilled in Vine Leaves

SERVES 4

12 vine leaves preserved
in brine
12 fresh sardines, cleaned but
heads and tails left intact

salt and freshly ground black
pepper
¼ cup olive oil
lemon wedges, to serve

Rinse vine leaves and pat dry with paper towels.

Wipe sardines and pat dry with paper towels. Sprinkle with salt and pepper, then wrap each sardine in a vine leaf, leaving head and tail exposed. Brush with olive oil.

Preheat oven grill or barbecue to high. Chargrill sardine bundles for about 5 minutes, turning once, until cooked.

Serve immediately with lemon wedges.

✕ A scoop of garlicky alioli (page 238) goes well with this dish and, of course, some fresh, crusty bread. Preserved vine leaves are sold in jars and are available at most supermarkets and delis.

Prawn Fritters

SERVES 4–6

1½ cups chickpea flour
½ teaspoon sweet Spanish
   paprika
salt
2 spring onions (or scallions),
   finely chopped
1 tablespoon chopped fresh,
   flat-leaf parsley

9 ounces freshly cooked
   prawns, shelled, deveined
   and roughly chopped
water, to form batter
olive oil for deep-frying
lemon wedges and extra
   paprika, to serve

Put flour, paprika, a good pinch of salt, spring onions, parsley and 1 cup water in a bowl and mix to form a batter. Cover and refrigerate for 1 hour.

Place prawns in a food processor or blender and pulse until roughly minced (with a little texture). Add to batter and mix well.

Pour olive oil into heavy-based fry pan to a depth of about ¾-inch over medium heat. When olive oil is hot, drop in spoonfuls of the batter to make small fritters. Cook for about 2 minutes, turning once, until golden brown. Only cook a few fritters at a time, as the olive oil needs to stay hot. Remove fritters from pan with a slotted spoon, drain on paper towels and keep warm until all fritters are cooked. Serve with lemon wedges and an extra sprinkling of paprika.

Crumbed Mussels

SERVES 4–6

water, to cook mussels
3 pounds 5 ounces fresh
    mussels, scrubbed and
    debearded
2 tablespoons olive oil
1 clove garlic, chopped
1 tablespoon tomato paste
1 tablespoon freshly squeezed
    lemon juice
pinch of hot Spanish paprika
2 tablespoons finely chopped
    fresh flat-leaf parsley

salt and freshly ground black
    pepper
1 tablespoon butter
1 cup dry breadcrumbs

SAUCE

1½ tablespoons butter
2 tablespoons plain flour
3 tablespoons milk
3 tablespoons fish stock

Pour 2 cups water into a large saucepan and bring to a boil over high heat. Add cleaned mussels, cover and cook for 4–5 minutes. Discard any mussels that do not open. Strain liquid from saucepan and reserve about ½ cup.

Remove mussels from their shells (save the shells), and chop the flesh.

Heat 1 tablespoon olive oil in a non-stick fry pan over medium heat, add garlic and cook for 1–2 minutes. Add tomato paste, reserved mussel liquid, lemon juice, paprika and parsley. Cook, stirring, until the mixture just comes to a boil.

Add mussel meat, reduce heat and simmer for 2–3 minutes. Season with salt, if needed, and pepper. Spoon mixture into the reserved mussel shells.

Preheat the oven broiler to hot.

Make the sauce: melt butter in a small saucepan over low heat, add flour and cook, stirring, for 1 minute. Pour in the milk and fish stock, stirring continuously, then reduce heat and simmer for 2–3 minutes until thick and smooth. Season with salt and pepper. Let cool a little.

Spoon sauce over mussel mixture in the shells and place shells on a baking sheet.

Melt butter and remaining oil in small fry pan. Add breadcrumbs and fry until crisp, then sprinkle on top of each filled mussel shell. Place the filled mussel shells under the broiler, until the sauce is bubbling and heated through.

Transfer to a serving platter and serve hot.

Marinated Fish

Escabeche

SERVES 4

2 pounds 3 ounces fresh tuna, cut into ¾-inch slices
½ cup all-purpose flour
¾ cup olive oil, plus extra for sautéing and drizzling over tuna
1 onion, thinly sliced
2 red bell peppers, deseeded and thinly sliced
1 clove garlic, crushed
½ cup pitted green olives, sliced

2 tablespoons baby capers, drained
½ teaspoon sweet Spanish paprika
2 tablespoons finely chopped fresh flat-leaf parsley
½ cup sherry vinegar
1 teaspoon salt
freshly ground black pepper
extra chopped parsley, to serve (optional)

Lightly dust tuna slices with flour and shake off any excess.

Heat 3 tablespoons of the olive oil in a large fry pan over medium–high heat. Add half the fish pieces and sauté for about 4 minutes, turning once, until lightly browned. Drain on paper towels. Cook and drain remaining tuna, then set aside.

Add a little extra olive oil to the fry pan if needed. Sauté onion and red bell peppers over medium heat for 7–8 minutes, until soft and just starting to brown. Add garlic, olives, capers, paprika, parsley, vinegar, salt and pepper, and stir to combine.

Put a layer of tuna in a shallow ceramic or glass casserole dish. Top with a layer of onion mixture, then repeat layers (ending with the onion mixture). Drizzle with any remaining olive oil. Cover and refrigerate for at least 8 hours.

Serve scattered with chopped parsley, if desired.

Tuna Toasts
Tostados de atun

SERVES 4–6

4 slices sourdough bread,
    crusts removed
3½ ounces canned tuna in
    water, drained
3 tablespoons good-quality
    mayonnaise
1 tablespoon baby capers,
    drained
freshly ground black pepper
sweet Spanish paprika,
    to serve

Toast bread, then cut each slice into strips 1¼ inches wide.

Place tuna in a bowl and mash well. Stir through the mayonnaise and capers and season with a good twist of black pepper.

Spread tuna mixture over the toasted bread slices, sprinkle with paprika and serve immediately.

✕ Tostado means toasted, while tostada is the name for a particular dish.

Monkfish with Saffron & Almonds

SERVES 4–6

2 pounds 3 ounces skinless
  monkfish fillets, cut into
  even-sized pieces
2 tablespoons olive oil
2 cloves garlic, crushed
3 red bell peppers, deseeded
  and cut into strips

1 cup fish stock
¾ cup blanched almonds,
  toasted and finely ground
½ teaspoon saffron threads,
  crumbled
½ teaspoon salt
freshly ground black pepper

Preheat oven to 350°F. Lightly oil a lidded baking dish, add fish and season lightly with salt and pepper. Cover, place in preheated oven and bake for 10–15 minutes. Remove from oven and transfer fish pieces to a plate (reserve the juices for sauce).

Heat olive oil in a heavy-based saucepan over medium heat. Add garlic and red bell peppers, and sauté for 2–3 minutes until starting to soften. Reduce heat and cook for an additional 10 minutes. Add fish juices, stock, ground almonds, saffron, salt and pepper, stir to combine, then simmer for 5 minutes. Pour mixture into a food processor or blender and blend.

Return sauce to the saucepan, add fish fillets, cover and simmer for 5 minutes or until fish is heated through. Serve immediately.

✕ Substitutes for monkfish include mahi mahi, red snapper or lobster.

Baby Clams with Chorizo

SERVES 4

2 tablespoons olive oil
2 cloves garlic, crushed
4 ounces cured chorizo
   sausage, diced
1 pound 12 ounces canned
   chopped tomatoes
1 fresh red chili pepper,
   deseeded and chopped

2 pounds 3 ounces baby clams,
   scrubbed
salt
2 tablespoons chopped fresh
   cilantro
bread, to soak up sauce

Heat olive oil in a large saucepan over medium heat, add garlic and chorizo and cook for 2–3 minutes until chorizo starts to brown. Add tomatoes and red chili pepper, bring to a boil, then reduce heat and simmer for 15 minutes, until sauce thickens.

Add clams to sauce and cook over low–medium heat, stirring once or twice, for about 5 minutes. Discard any clams that have not opened.

Check for seasoning, adding salt if needed. Serve immediately, sprinkled with the cilantro, and offer plenty of fresh bread for soaking up the sauce.

Trout with Jamon

SERVES 4–6

4 small trout (about 9 ounces
each), cleaned
6 thin slices jamon
(or prosciutto)
freshly ground black pepper
salt

½ cup all-purpose flour
4 tablespoons butter
2 tablespoons olive oil
finely chopped fresh flat-leaf
parsley for garnish
lemon wedges, to serve

Rinse trout and pat dry, inside and out, with paper towels.

Place one slice of ham in the cavity of each trout, season with pepper and secure opening with a toothpick. Finely chop the remaining ham.

Season flour with salt and pepper, then dust the trout lightly with flour and shake off any excess. Heat butter and olive oil in a large non-stick fry pan over medium heat until sizzling. Add trout (two at a time) and fry for 5–6 minutes on each side. Turn carefully, using a spatula to keep fish from breaking. When cooked, remove to warmed plates.

Add chopped ham to the pan and sauté over high heat until crisp. Spoon crisped ham and the pan juices over the trout, scatter with parsley and serve with lemon wedges.

Baked Sardines

SERVES 4–6

oil, to prepare baking dish
3 cloves garlic, crushed
1 cup fine dry breadcrumbs
2 tablespoons finely chopped
  fresh flat-leaf parsley
salt and freshly ground black
  pepper

2 pounds 3 ounces fresh
  sardines, filleted
$1/3$ cup olive oil
lemon wedges, to serve

Preheat oven to 350°F. Lightly oil a baking dish.

Mix garlic, breadcrumbs and parsley in a bowl with some salt and pepper. Pat sardine fillets dry, brush with olive oil, then dip into the crumb mixture. Lay the fillets in a single layer in prepared baking dish and bake in preheated oven for 10–15 minutes.

Serve hot, with lemon wedges.

Scallops in White Wine

SERVES 4

oil, to prepare baking dish

20 medium-sized scallops, rinsed and drained

2 tablespoons freshly squeezed lemon juice

3 tablespoons olive oil

1 onion, finely chopped

2 ounces jamon (or prosciutto), chopped

1 cup dry white wine

pinch of saffron threads, crumbled

1 teaspoon sweet Spanish paprika

1 tablespoon chopped fresh chives

½ cup dry breadcrumbs

salt and freshly ground black pepper

extra chopped chives, to serve

Preheat oven to 400°F. Lightly oil a baking dish. Place the scallops in the dish in a single layer, pour the lemon juice over, then cover and refrigerate.

Heat olive oil in a fry pan over medium heat. Add onion and ham and sauté for about 10 minutes, until onion is softened. Add wine and saffron, and cook for an additional 5 minutes or so, until sauce is reduced. Stir in paprika, chives and breadcrumbs. Season to taste with salt and freshly ground black pepper.

While sauce is still warm, spoon over the scallops. Place in preheated oven and bake for about 5 minutes until golden. Scatter with extra chives and serve immediately.

Squid with Peas

SERVES 4

2 pounds 3 ounces squid,
  cleaned
4 tablespoons olive oil
4 cloves garlic, sliced
2 pounds 3 ounces juicy
  tomatoes, peeled and
  roughly chopped
2 tablespoons finely chopped
  fresh flat-leaf parsley

½ cup dry white wine
12 ounces peas, fresh or frozen
salt and freshly ground black
  pepper
2 tablespoons chopped fresh
  mint leaves, to serve

Cut the squid tubes into ¾-inch rings, but leave the tentacles whole (unless they are very long).

Heat the olive oil in a large fry pan over medium–high heat. Add garlic and sauté for 1–2 minutes then add squid and sauté for another 1–2 minutes, until it has a little color. Add tomatoes, parsley and white wine, bring to a boil, reduce heat to very low and simmer, uncovered, for 20 minutes, stirring occasionally.

Add peas and cook for another 3–5 minutes, until peas are tender and sauce has thickened. Check seasoning, adding salt and pepper to taste. Scatter with chopped mint leaves and serve immediately.

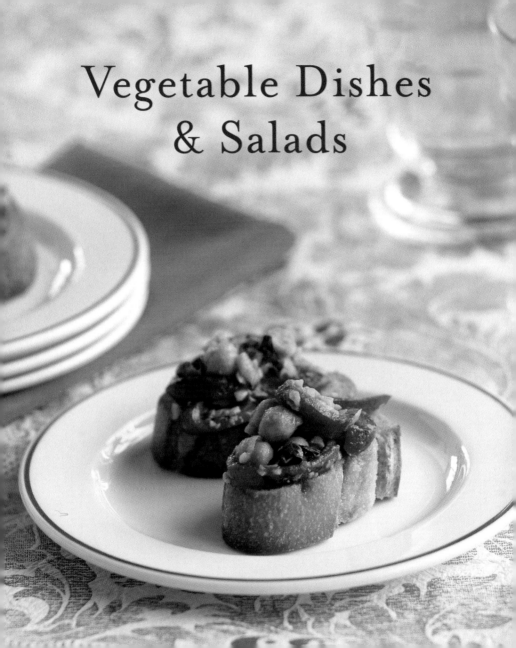

Vegetable Dishes
& Salads

Vegetables in Spain are often served before a main meat or seafood dish, but are commonly (especially if jamon, eggs or sausage are added) served as the main course. The Mediterranean staples — tomatoes, bell peppers, onions and garlic — fresh and dried beans, and seasonal treats such as wild asparagus, are special favorites. Potatoes are also on every menu and are cooked in all manner of ways; from the popular tapa, patatas bravas, to side dishes and tortillas.

Traditionally salads are simple — combinations of sun-ripened tomatoes, cucumber and bell pepper, fresh greens, plump olives — all glistening with luscious local extra-virgin olive oil.

< SPICY CHICKPEAS WITH ROASTED BELL PEPPERS (PAGE 114)

Spicy Chickpeas
with Roasted Bell Peppers

SERVES 6

12 thick slices bread from
    baguette
¾ cup olive oil
juice of 1 lemon
2 cloves garlic, crushed
2 teaspoons hot Spanish
    paprika
14 ounces canned chickpeas,
    rinsed and drained

4 roasted and marinated bell
    peppers (page 245),
    sliced into strips
salt and freshly ground black
    pepper
2 tablespoons chopped fresh
    mint

Preheat oven to 300°F.

Brush bread slices with some of the olive oil, place on baking sheet and bake
in preheated oven for 6–8 minutes, until lightly toasted.

Put the remaining olive oil, lemon juice, garlic and paprika in a medium-sized
bowl and whisk to combine. Add chickpeas, toss to coat with dressing and
lightly crush the chickpeas to a textured mixture. Stir in marinated bell pepper
strips and season with salt and pepper.

Pile chickpea and bell pepper mixture on toasted bread, sprinkle with mint,
and serve.

Potatoes with Garlic Mayo
Patatas alioli

SERVES 4–6

olive oil for frying
6 medium-sized potatoes,
   peeled and cut into bite-
   sized cubes
alioli (page 238)

Heat about 1½-inches olive oil in a deep fry pan or heavy-based saucepan over medium–high heat, until hot. When the olive oil is ready, carefully add potatoes and deep-fry until brown and crisp. Remove with a slotted spoon and drain on paper towels.

Place potatoes in a warmed serving dish, spoon alioli over and serve.

Spicy Potatoes

Patatas bravas

SERVES 4–6

6 medium-sized potatoes, peeled and cut into bite-sized cubes
water, to boil potatoes
3 tablespoons olive oil
2 cloves garlic, chopped
1 small onion, finely chopped
1 (14-ounce) can crushed tomatoes

1 tablespoon hot Spanish paprika
¼ teaspoon cayenne pepper
1 bay leaf
salt and freshly ground black pepper
2 tablespoons finely chopped fresh flat-leaf parsley, to serve

Preheat oven to 425°F. Line a baking sheet with parchment (baking) paper.

Boil potato cubes until just soft. Drain well. Put potatoes on the baking sheet and drizzle with about 2 tablespoons of olive oil and bake for 15–20 minutes, turning once or twice, until quite crisp and golden.

While potatoes are cooking, heat remaining olive oil in a saucepan over medium heat. Add garlic and onion and fry for 2–3 minutes until softened. Add tomatoes, paprika, cayenne and bay leaf and stir. Cover and simmer for 10–15 minutes, until thickened and reduced. Season to taste with salt and pepper.

Put baked potatoes in a warmed dish. Remove bay leaf from tomato sauce and pour sauce over potatoes.

Scatter parsley on top and serve immediately.

✄ In small quantities, Patatas bravas are a popular tapa. If you prefer you can deep-fry the potatoes instead of baking them (see instructions on page 115).

Stuffed Tomatoes

Tomatoes rellenos

SERVES 8

8 medium-sized vine-ripened
   tomatoes
boiling water and ice water, to
   skin tomatoes
4 hard-boiled eggs, shelled
½ cup mayonnaise or alioli
   (page 238)

½ cup fresh breadcrumbs
salt and freshly ground black
   pepper
8–10 fresh basil leaves, torn
1 tablespoon toasted pine nuts
2 tablespoons pitted, sliced
   black Spanish olives

Cut a small cross on the bottom of each tomato. Place tomatoes in boiling water for 30 seconds, then remove and plunge them at once into iced water (to stop the cooking). Using a sharp knife, peel away the skin.

Slice the tops off the tomatoes. Use the tops as "lids" or discard if the tomatoes are fairly small. Scoop out tomato flesh, using a teaspoon or melon-baller, and place tomatoes upside down to drain. (Save the tomato flesh and use in a sauce or soup.)

Mash the eggs with the mayonnaise, breadcrumbs, salt and pepper. Then stir through the basil leaves, pine nuts and olives. Spoon mixture into the tomato shells, pressing down, to fill the cavities, then replace lids (if using). Serve at room temperature.

Lentils with Mushrooms & Leeks

SERVES 4–6

1 pound 2 ounces dried brown lentils, rinsed

7 ounces unsliced bacon, or ham hock

water, to cover lentils and bacon or ham hock

2 tablespoons olive oil

1 small onion, chopped

2 medium-sized leeks (white parts only), finely sliced

9 ounces white button mushrooms, sliced

2 large vine-ripened tomatoes, peeled and chopped

sprig of fresh rosemary

salt and freshly ground black pepper

2 tablespoons anise liqueur (such as Anis del Mono, or Pernod)

Put the lentils in a large, heavy-based saucepan with the bacon or ham hock and enough water to cover. Bring to a boil, skim the surface if necessary, then reduce heat, cover and simmer for 35–40 minutes until lentils are soft but not mushy. Check occasionally to make sure there is enough water.

When lentils are cooked, drain and remove bacon or hock.

Heat olive oil in a large, non-stick fry pan over medium heat. Add onion and leeks, and cook, stirring occasionally for 5–6 minutes, until softened. Add mushrooms, tomatoes, and rosemary, and cook for 10 minutes until the vegetables start to soften into a sauce. >

Roughly dice the bacon, or, if using a ham hock, scrape any meat from the bone and gently pull apart the meat. Add meat and lentils to the pan, stir, cover and simmer over low heat for an additional 10 minutes. Season with salt and pepper, then stir the liqueur through the sauce, and serve.

✕ Black pudding (*morcilla*) is often added to this dish. If using, cut about 7 ounces of the sausage into thick slices and add to the fry pan with the lentils.

Russian Salad
Ensaladilla Rusa

SERVES 4

1 pound 9 ounces small, waxy
  potatoes
2 small carrots, cut in half
water, to boil potatoes and
  carrots
9 ounces peas, fresh or frozen
water, to boil and refresh peas
2 hard-boiled eggs,
  shelled and quartered

2 tablespoons finely chopped
  fresh chives
²/₃ cup good-quality
  mayonnaise
salt and freshly ground black
  pepper

Boil the potatoes and carrots until tender, then drain. Allow to cool, then peel and cut into small cubes. Place in a serving bowl.

Boil the peas for a few minutes until cooked. Refresh in iced water (to stop the cooking and retain their bright-green color), then drain and add to the cooked potatoes. Add the hard-boiled eggs and chives, and then carefully stir the mayonnaise through until everything is lightly coated. Season with salt and pepper to taste. Cover and refrigerate until ready to serve.

✕ This 'Russian' salad is a popular tapa in Spain. Canned tuna is often added.

Basque-style Eggs
Piperada

SERVES 2

2 tablespoons olive oil
2 cloves garlic, crushed
½ red onion, thinly sliced
2 red bell peppers, deseeded
    and cut into slices
4 large, vine-ripened
    tomatoes, peeled and
    chopped
1 sprig fresh thyme

salt and freshly ground black
    pepper
4 eggs
1 tablespoon finely chopped
    fresh flat-leaf parsley
croutons (see note on page 63),
    to serve

Heat olive oil in a large lidded non-stick fry pan over medium heat. Add garlic and onion and sauté for 2–3 minutes until softened. Add red bell peppers and cook for another 2–3 minutes, stirring occasionally. Add tomatoes, thyme, salt and pepper. Stir, cover, reduce heat and simmer for 10 minutes or until tomatoes are cooked.

Break eggs into a bowl, being careful not to break the yolks, then slide gently, one by one, over the tomato mixture. Cover pan again and cook until the egg whites are set but the yolks are still a little runny.

When eggs are ready, sprinkle with parsley and croutons, and serve immediately.

✕ Piperada is based on tomatoes and sweet bell peppers.

Baby Leek Salad

SERVES 4

16 baby leeks
water, to boil and refresh leeks
3 tablespoons extra-virgin
   olive oil
2 tablespoons sherry vinegar
1 clove garlic, crushed
salt and freshly ground black
   pepper

2 hard-boiled eggs, shelled
   and finely chopped
½ cup walnuts, toasted
1 tablespoon chopped fresh
   cilantro

Trim tops and bottoms of leeks and slit lengthwise to the center. Boil the leeks in a small amount of water for 3–4 minutes. Drain, refresh under cold water and drain again.

To make dressing, whisk extra-virgin olive oil with vinegar and garlic, then season with salt and pepper.

Arrange leeks on a serving platter and pour the dressing over. Scatter the chopped egg, walnuts and cilantro on top and serve at room temperature.

※ If you can't buy baby leeks, use instead the smallest leeks you can find, but trim off the green ends, which can be tough.

Cauliflower with Garlic & Almond Picada

SERVES 4

1 small cauliflower, cut into florets
boiling water, to cook cauliflower
4 cloves garlic, roughly chopped
3 tablespoons chopped fresh flat-leaf parsley
1 teaspoon salt flakes (delicate finishing salt)
¼ cup olive oil
½ cup sliced almonds
2 teaspoons sweet Spanish paprika
1 tablespoon dry sherry

Cook cauliflower in boiling water for 4–5 minutes until tender. Drain (reserving a few tablespoons of cooking liquid), transfer to a heated serving dish and keep warm.

Pound garlic, parsley and salt in a mortar to form a paste. Stir in a few tablespoons of reserved cooking liquid and half the olive oil, and mix well.

Heat remaining olive oil in a non-stick fry pan over medium heat. Add sliced almonds and stir until they are lightly toasted. Reduce heat, add paprika and sherry, stir, then stir in the garlic paste.

Spoon over the cauliflower and serve immediately.

※ A *picada* is a little like an Italian pesto. This version provides a piquant contrast to the cauliflower.

Spinach with Olives & Pine Nuts

3 tablespoons olive oil

2 cloves garlic, sliced

2 spring onions, chopped

½ cup sliced black Spanish olives

1 pound 2 ounces baby spinach leaves, rinsed

¼ cup pine nuts, toasted

freshly ground black pepper

extra-virgin olive oil, to drizzle

Heat olive oil in a large non-stick fry pan over medium heat, add garlic and spring onions, and sauté for 1–2 minutes until softened. Add olives and stir to heat through. Add spinach leaves and toss for a few minutes until just wilted. Drain off any excess liquid.

Add pine nuts, season with freshly ground pepper, drizzle with a little extra-virgin olive oil and serve.

Golden Saffron Potatoes

SERVES 4

2 pounds 14 ounces medium-sized potatoes, peeled and halved
cold water, to cover potatoes
pinch of saffron threads, crumbled

2 tablespoons olive oil
½ teaspoon ground turmeric
salt and freshly ground black pepper

Preheat oven to 350°F.

Put potatoes into a large saucepan, cover with cold water, add saffron and bring to a boil over a high heat. Reduce heat and boil for about 10 minutes, until almost tender. Drain well.

Return potatoes to saucepan, add olive oil and turmeric, and season with salt and pepper. Put lid on pan and toss potatoes to coat and roughen edges.

Place potatoes onto non-stick baking sheet or pan and roast in preheated oven for about 40 minutes, until crisp and golden.

Greens, Valdeon Cheese & Smoked Almonds

SERVES 6

1 butterhead, Bibb or Boston
  lettuce, leaves torn into
  bite-sized pieces
2 cups arugula leaves, torn
  into bite-sized pieces
7 ounces Valdeon blue cheese
  (or other crumbly blue
  cheese)

3 tablespoons extra-virgin
  olive oil
2 tablespoons sherry vinegar
freshly ground black pepper
3 ounces smoked almonds,
  roughly chopped

Put lettuce and arugula into a bowl and crumble cheese on top.

Whisk extra-virgin olive oil, vinegar and pepper to make a dressing. Pour over salad and toss lightly. Scatter almonds on top and serve immediately.

※ If Spanish Valdeon cheese is unavailable, try another crumbly blue cheese with 'bite', such as Gorgonzola. Smoked almonds can be found in nut shops and most supermarkets.

Tomato & Cucumber Salad

Pipirrana

SERVES 4–6

2 pounds vine-ripened
   tomatoes, peeled and
   chopped
1 red bell pepper, deseeded
   and finely chopped
1 small red onion,
   finely chopped

2 English (seedless)
   cucumbers, thinly sliced
½ cup pitted black Spanish
   olives
½ cup sherry vinaigrette
   (page 247)

Place vegetables and olives in a bowl and toss lightly. Pour vinaigrette over the salad and toss again to coat. Cover, and refrigerate for an hour before serving.

Serve chilled.

※ This is a popular salad in Andalusia. Chopped hard-boiled eggs and tuna in oil – two favorite Spanish ingredients – are sometimes added. Serve with crusty bread for a casual lunch.

White Anchovy, Fennel & Lemon Salad
Ensalada de boquerones

SERVES 6–8

¹/₃ cup extra-virgin olive oil
2 tablespoons red-wine vinegar
freshly ground black pepper
7 ounces arugula leaves
2 baby fennel bulbs, sliced as
    thinly as possible (set aside
    the leafy fronds for garnish)

1 small red onion,
    sliced as thinly as possible
2 wedges preserved lemon,
    skin removed, diced
8 ounces white anchovies

Whisk extra-virgin olive oil, vinegar and pepper together, to make the dressing.

Put arugula, fennel, onion and preserved lemon in a serving bowl, pour dressing over and toss to combine. Arrange anchovies on top, then scatter with chopped fennel fronds and serve.

※ Preserved lemons are available in jars, from specialty food stores and delis. They are more mellow and less acidic than fresh lemons. You can replace the white anchovies with flaked, smoked trout.

Asparagus & Orange Salad

SERVES 4

8 ounces asparagus spears
water, to boil and blanch
 asparagus
2 oranges
1 butterhead, Bibb or Boston
 lettuce
2 vine-ripened tomatoes,
 peeled and quartered

1½ tablespoons extra-virgin
 olive oil
2 teaspoons white-wine
 vinegar
salt and freshly ground black
 pepper
1 tablespoon chopped fresh
 flat-leaf parsley, for garnish

Trim asparagus and cut into 2-inch lengths. Bring a small pot of water to a boil and blanch the asparagus for 3–4 minutes, until just tender. Drain. Refresh in iced water to stop the cooking process.

Finely grate the zest of 1 orange. Peel the other orange and pull both oranges apart into segments, removing all pith and membranes.

Place lettuce leaves, tomatoes, orange segments and drained asparagus in a salad bowl.

Whisk extra-virgin olive oil, vinegar and orange zest together to make a dressing, seasoning with salt and pepper. Pour dressing over salad and scatter parsley on top. Toss gently and serve immediately.

Slow-roasted Baby Beets with Goat Curd & Hazelnuts

SERVES 4

3 tablespoons extra-virgin olive oil

1 tablespoon red-wine vinegar

salt and freshly ground black pepper

2 bunches baby beets, scrubbed and trimmed

13 ounces goat cheese curd or soft goat cheese

½ cup hazelnuts, roasted and chopped

½ handful fresh mint leaves

extra-virgin olive oil, to drizzle

Preheat oven to 325°F.

Whisk olive oil and vinegar together and season with salt and pepper. Set aside.

Lay half of the baby beets in a single layer on aluminum foil, then fold foil over to seal. Do the same with the remaining beets. Place both bundles in a baking dish and bake in preheated oven for 30–40 minutes, until tender when pierced with tip of a small knife.

When beets are cooked, allow to cool a little, then rub off the skins. **>**

Arrange on a serving platter or individual plates and sprinkle with bits of goat cheese curd or soft goat cheese. Pour a little of the dressing over and scatter the hazelnuts on top.

Sprinkle with fresh mint leaves and an extra drizzle of olive oil, and serve.

※ Use rubber gloves when rubbing off beet skins otherwise your fingers will be stained pink.

※ Fresh goat cheese is like fromage blanc or bucheron, but made with goat milk.

Onion & Orange Salad

SERVES 6

2 tablespoons raisins
boiling water, to soak raisins
3 oranges, peeled
1 small red onion, thinly
   sliced
12 pitted black olives, sliced
^{1}/$_3$ cup extra-virgin olive oil
1 teaspoon Dijon mustard

2 tablespoons lemon juice
salt and freshly ground black
   pepper
2 tablespoons sliced almonds,
   lightly toasted
a few torn mint leaves,
   for garnish

Put raisins in a small bowl or cup, cover with boiling water and soak for 20 minutes. Drain.

Use a sharp knife to cut oranges into segments, making sure to remove all the pith and membranes. Arrange orange segments on a platter and scatter onion, olives and raisins on top.

Whisk together extra-virgin olive oil, mustard and lemon juice, and season with salt and pepper. Pour dressing over the salad and toss gently. Sprinkle toasted almonds and mint on top, cover, and refrigerate for 1 hour before serving. Serve chilled.

✕ Buy good-quality black olives and slice them yourself – many ready-sliced olives are lacking in flavor.

Chargrilled Catalan Salad
Escalivada

SERVES 4

4 small eggplants, halved
1 red onion, halved
4 red bell peppers, deseeded
   and then halved lengthwise
2 large vine-ripened tomatoes,
   halved
about ½ cup olive oil

2 tablespoons freshly squeezed
   lemon juice
2 cloves garlic, crushed
salt and freshly ground black
   pepper

Preheat grill to hot.

Brush vegetables with some of the olive oil and grill for 15–20 minutes until they are soft and the edges blackened (some will cook more quickly than others). Remove vegetables from the grill and allow to cool.

Slice red bell peppers into strips. Remove ends from eggplant and cut flesh into strips. Cut tomatoes into quarters and remove cores. Cut onion into thick slices. Arrange all the vegetables on a serving dish.

To make dressing, whisk remaining olive oil with the lemon juice and garlic, then season with salt and pepper. Pour over vegetables and toss gently to combine.

Serve at room temperature.

✕ Escalivar means "to cook in hot ashes". The vegetables in this Catalan dish are often served with grilled meats.

Green Beans with Almonds & Cumin

SERVES 4

1 pound green beans, tops and
ends removed
water, to blanch green beans
2 tablespoons extra-virgin
olive oil
1 ounce sliced almonds

1 teaspoon cumin seeds
1 teaspoon hot Spanish
paprika
extra-virgin olive oil, to serve
salt flakes (delicate finishing
salt)

Bring a small pot of water to a boil. Blanch the green beans for 4–5 minutes, until just soft but still green. Drain.

Heat extra-virgin olive oil in a fry pan over medium–high heat. Fry almonds for about 30 seconds, then add cumin seeds and fry for a few seconds more. Remove from heat and stir in paprika.

Add cooked green beans to the pan, toss to combine. Drizzle with a little extra-virgin olive oil, add salt flakes to taste, and serve.

Castilian Red Cabbage

SERVES 4–6

1¾ pounds red cabbage (about 1 whole cabbage), finely shredded

boiling water, to almost cover cabbage

2 tablespoons olive oil

3 cloves garlic, sliced

1 small chorizo sausage (about 1¾ ounces), cut into small cubes

3½ ounces salted pork belly, chopped into small cubes

2 tablespoons red-wine vinegar

Put shredded cabbage in a large saucepan, pour over enough boiling water to almost cover, then cook over medium heat for about 10 minutes until cabbage has softened. Drain well.

Heat olive oil in a non-stick fry pan over medium heat. Add garlic, chorizo and pork belly, and sauté for about 5 minutes, until meat is starting to brown. Add cabbage and stir to combine. Reduce heat and simmer for 15 minutes, stirring occasionally, until cabbage is soft. Stir in red-wine vinegar and cook for another 5 minutes.

Serve immediately.

✕ Ask your butcher or deli for salted pork belly. If it's not available, pancetta is an acceptable substitute.

Paellas & Other Plates to Share

Large meals in Spain tend to be hearty and substantial — often based around meat and potatoes, beans or rice — with many regional specialties incorporating ingredients and influences unique to the area. While many non-Spaniards think of paella as emblematic of Spanish food, it is, in fact a regional speciality specific to Valencia. Cocido Mardrileno (page 172) — a robust, chickpea-based hotpot — is more widely considered one of Spain's national dishes.

In Spain, paella is not often cooked at home — it is a dish cooked for festive occasions, or at restaurants. Home stoves cannot usually provide enough heat for the wide pan, so finishing the dish in the oven ensures the rice is cooked through. As with risotto, paella rice should be a little firm when cooked; unlike a risotto, paella should be stirred as little as possible. The best paellas form a delicious crust (socarrat) on the underside.

‹ PAELLA WITH RED BELL PEPPER (PAGE 148)

Paella with Red Bell Pepper

SERVES 4

3 tablespoons olive oil

1 onion, chopped

3 cloves garlic, chopped

2 red bell peppers, deseeded
and sliced

4 large, vine-ripened
tomatoes, peeled and
chopped

12 ounces short-grain paella
or risotto rice

4 cups hot chicken or fish stock

12 ounces raw (green) prawns,
shelled and deveined

8 ounces peas,
fresh or frozen

a few threads of saffron,
crumbled

½ teaspoon hot Spanish
paprika

sprig of fresh rosemary

salt and freshly ground black
pepper to taste

lemon wedges, to serve

alioli (page 238), to serve
(optional)

Heat olive oil in a paella pan or a large, wide fry pan. Add onion and garlic and cook for 5 minutes, stirring, over low heat until onions start to caramelize. Add red bell peppers and cook for 1–2 minutes. Add tomatoes and cook for about 15 minutes over low heat, stirring occasionally, until the tomatoes thicken to form a sauce.

Add rice to pan, stir to coat in the sauce, and cook for 5 minutes. Slowly add the hot stock, along with the prawns, peas, saffron, paprika, rosemary, salt and pepper. Stir once, bring to a boil, then cover and simmer over low heat for about 15–20 minutes until stock is absorbed, stirring the dish as little as possible. If there is too much liquid near the end of the cooking time, increase heat to boil it away, but prevent scorching.

When rice is cooked, turn off heat, cover pan with clean kitchen towel and leave for 5 minutes.

Serve with lemon wedges and a bowl of alioli on the side, if desired.

※ Calasparra and Bomba are the best-known Spanish rice varieties for paella, but if they are not available choose a good-quality short-grain rice, such as arborio.

Paella with Chicken & Rabbit
Paella a la Valenciana

SERVES 6–8

2 cups chicken or veal stock
water, to infuse herbs and
    saffron
2 sprigs each fresh thyme and
    rosemary
a few saffron threads,
    crumbled
1 pound 10 ounces chicken
    legs and thighs
1 pound 10 ounces rabbit
    pieces
salt and freshly ground black
    pepper
5 tablespoons olive oil
1 green bell pepper, deseeded
    and finely chopped

1 brown-skinned onion, finely
    chopped
6 cloves garlic, crushed
8 ounces green beans, halved
2 vine-ripened tomatoes,
    peeled and chopped
8 ounces peas, fresh or frozen
3 tablespoons chopped fresh
    flat-leaf parsley
2 teaspoons sweet Spanish
    paprika
3 cups short-grain paella
    or risotto rice
extra chopped fresh flat-leaf
    parsley and lemon wedges,
    to serve

Put stock, 4 cups water, herb sprigs and saffron in a small saucepan and simmer over low heat for 20 minutes to infuse.

Debone chicken and rabbit and cut into bite-sized pieces. Season with salt and pepper.

Preheat oven to 400°F.

In a paella pan or ovenproof fry pan approximately 18 inches wide, heat 3 tablespoons of the olive oil over medium–high heat. Sauté chicken and rabbit pieces in batches for about 5 minutes, until lightly browned but not cooked through. Set aside.

Add green bell pepper, onion and garlic, and sauté until starting to soften. Add beans, and tomatoes and cook for about 2 minutes more, then stir in the peas, parsley and paprika. Add rice and stir to coat, return chicken and rabbit to the pan and strain in the hot stock. Bring to a boil, cook for 5 minutes without stirring, then reduce heat and cook for a few more minutes until most, but not all, of the liquid is absorbed. Check that the meat is cooked, and add extra seasoning if needed.

Place pan in preheated oven and cook, uncovered, for 10–12 minutes until rice is cooked. Remove from oven, cover pan with a clean kitchen towel and leave for 5–10 minutes to absorb any extra moisture.

Scatter with chopped parsley and serve direct from the pan, with lemon wedges on the side.

Seafood Paella
Paella a la marinera

SERVES 6–8

water, to steam mussels
24 small mussels, scrubbed
    and debearded
a few threads of saffron
warm water, to soak saffron
1 pound 9 ounces firm,
    white-fleshed fish fillets
    (use at least 2 varieties)
1 pound small or baby squid
    with tentacles, cleaned
18 large raw (green) prawns,
    unshelled
sea salt
6 cloves garlic, crushed
1 tablespoon chopped fresh
    thyme
2 tablespoons chopped fresh
    flat-leaf parsley

2 teaspoons sweet Spanish
    paprika
2 pinches ground cayenne
    pepper
water and/or olive oil, to make
    spice paste
6 cups fish stock
12 tablespoons olive oil
1 red onion, chopped
2 red bell peppers, deseeded
    and finely chopped
2 vine-ripened tomatoes,
    peeled and chopped
3 cups short-grain paella
    or risotto rice
lemon wedges, to serve
aioli (page 238), to serve
    (optional)

Put 2 cups water in a large saucepan, add mussels, bring to a boil, cover and steam for about 5 minutes or until shells open. (Discard any mussels that did not open.) ➤

Remove the meat from half the mussels but keep the other half in shells.

Crumble saffron into a little warm water and let soak for about 5 minutes.

Cut fish fillets into ½-inch cubes. Cut squid into squares, but leave tentacles whole. Place fish, squid and prawns in a bowl, sprinkle with sea salt and leave for 15 minutes.

Put garlic, thyme, parsley, paprika, cayenne and a few drops of water in a mortar and pound to make a paste. Add a little more water or some olive oil if the mixture is very dry.

Heat stock, saffron and its soaking liquid in a saucepan over medium heat. Cover and keep hot.

Preheat oven to 400°F.

In a paella pan or ovenproof fry pan approximately 18 inches in diameter, heat 6 tablespoons olive oil over medium heat. Add fish, squid and prawns in batches and sauté until they have a little color, but are not fully cooked. Transfer to a warmed plate.

Add remaining olive oil, onion and red bell peppers to the pan and cook gently for 6–7 minutes until vegetables are softening and the onion is starting to caramelize. Increase heat, add chopped tomatoes and cook for a few minutes until they start to soften.

Add rice to pan and stir to coat. Pour in hot stock, bring mixture to a boil and cook for 5 minutes, without stirring. Add fish, squid and garlic paste and gently stir through. Continue to cook for a few minutes until most of the stock is absorbed. If the pan is larger than your burner, move the pan to distribute the heat so all the rice cooks (a heat diffuser is helpful). Check seasoning and add salt if needed.

Add mussel meat to rice, and arrange prawns and mussels in shells on top of rice. Place pan in preheated oven and cook for 8–10 minutes until rice and prawns are cooked (they will turn pink and opaque) and all liquid is absorbed.

Remove pan from oven. Cover with a clean kitchen towel and let rest for 5–10 minutes, to absorb any extra moisture.

Serve paella direct from the pan, with lemon wedges. (Provide bowls for the prawn and mussel shells.)

✖ Firm fish suitable for this paella include snapper, cod or tilapia, or a combination.

✖ A heat diffuser provides a layer of protection between the burner and the bottom of the pan, while it allows heat to permeate.

Spanish Omelette
Tortilla Espagnola

SERVES 6

4 medium-sized potatoes,
   peeled and halved
salted water, to boil potatoes
salt
1/3 cup olive oil
3 cloves garlic, crushed
1 red onion, thinly sliced

6 large eggs
salt and freshly ground black
   pepper
finely chopped fresh flat-leaf
   parsley and sweet Spanish
   paprika for garnish

Boil potatoes in salted water for 6–7 minutes until half cooked. Drain and cut into thick slices.

Heat olive oil in a large, heavy-based, non-stick fry pan over medium heat. When it is hot, add garlic and onion and fry for 2–3 minutes. Add potatoes and cook over low heat until potatoes are cooked through (but don't let them color).

Whisk eggs lightly and season well with salt and pepper. Pour egg mixture over potatoes in the fry pan and tip pan to make sure potatoes are well coated. Cover pan, and cook over low heat for 5–10 minutes until eggs are set. If you like the top to be browned, place under the broiler for just a minute or so, or slide tortilla onto a plate and then back into the pan to cook the other side.

Slide cooked tortilla onto a large plate, or serve direct from the pan, warm or cold, scattered with parsley and a sprinkle of paprika.

To serve as a tapa, cut into triangles or small squares.

✕ Tortilla Espagnola is a Spanish tortilla, a thick egg omelette made with potatoes and fried in olive oil, not a Mexican maize tortilla.

✕ In Spain, the potatoes are usually cooked in a very large quantity of oil until soft, which makes for a very rich tortilla. Par-boiling them first reduces the amount of oil needed and produces a lighter dish.

Chorizo Omelette
Tortilla al chorizo

SERVES 6–8

⅓ cup olive oil

7 ounces cured chorizo sausage, thinly sliced

1 red onion, thinly sliced

1 pound 5 ounces potatoes, very thinly sliced

6 eggs

1 cup grated manchego cheese (or other firm sheep milk cheese, such as pecorino)

salt and freshly ground black pepper

2 tablespoons chopped fresh cilantro

Heat 1 tablespoon of the olive oil in a non-stick fry pan over medium heat, then add chorizo and fry for a few minutes until lightly browned. Remove from the pan and set aside.

Heat a little more olive oil in the same pan and cook onion and potatoes, stirring, for 3–4 minutes. Reduce heat to low, cover and cook for 20 minutes, checking occasionally, until vegetables are softened.

In a bowl, whisk eggs with the grated cheese and season well with salt and pepper. Stir cilantro and cooked chorizo into the eggs, add onions and potatoes, and mix carefully.

Wipe pan, then heat remaining olive oil. Pour in egg mixture and cook over low heat until almost set, then place it under a hot broiler to brown the top. Serve hot or at room temperature.

Spanish Meatballs
Albondigas

MAKES ABOUT 30

10½ ounces minced beef or
  pork
½ cup dry breadcrumbs
1 teaspoon each ground
  cumin, coriander and
  nutmeg
3 cloves garlic
salt and freshly ground black
  pepper
5 tablespoons olive oil

1 red onion, finely chopped
1 (14-ounce) can crushed
  tomatoes
½ teaspoon sweet Spanish
  paprika
salt, to taste
all-purpose flour, for dusting
1 tablespoon chopped fresh
  flat-leaf parsley, to serve

Place the minced meat, breadcrumbs and spices in a bowl, crush 2 cloves of the garlic, add to the mixture and mix well. Season with salt and pepper, then refrigerate for an hour for flavors to develop.

Heat 3 tablespoons of the olive oil in a large non-stick fry pan or wide saucepan. Chop remaining garlic, add to pan with onion, and sauté for a few minutes, stirring occasionally. Add tomatoes, paprika, and salt to taste, then simmer (uncovered) for 10 minutes until sauce thickens. >

Remove the minced meat mixture from the refrigerator and roll into small balls. Dip into flour to dust lightly.

Heat remaining olive oil in a separate non-stick fry pan over medium heat. Fry meatballs for about 5 minutes, turning once or twice, until browned all over. Remove from pan, add to the sauce and simmer over medium heat for an additional 6–8 minutes (don't let the mixture boil). Stir through chopped parsley and serve.

Roast Pork Loin with Pedro Ximenez

SERVES 4

1 teaspoon sweet Spanish
   paprika
2 pounds 3 ounces pork loin,
   rinsed and patted dry
salt and freshly ground black
   pepper
½ pound sliced jamon

2 tablespoons olive oil
sprig of fresh rosemary
1 pound small onions
   or shallots, quartered
½ cup Pedro Ximenez sherry,
   plus extra for sauce
½ cup veal or chicken stock

Preheat oven to 350°F.

Rub paprika over the pork, then season well with salt and pepper. Wrap jamon around pork loin and tie in place with string.

Put olive oil in a large roasting pan over medium–high heat on top of the stove. When olive oil is hot, add pork and fry for 5–6 minutes until browned all over. Tuck rosemary sprig into the string. Add onions to the dish and fry until they start to brown. Pour sherry over pork, add stock, place pan in preheated oven and bake for 1 hour, basting the meat several times. **>**

When pork is cooked, remove from the oven, cover to keep it warm and set aside to rest for 5–10 minutes. Place the roasting pan over medium–high heat, add a little extra sherry to the juices and cook for 1 minute.

Remove string, cut pork into generous slices and arrange on a warmed serving platter with the onions. Spoon sauce over, and serve.

✕ If you cannot find Pedro Ximenez sherry, use a good-quality sweet, dark sherry, such as Moscatel (Muscat).

Salt Cod Baked with Potatoes

SERVES 4

1 pound 2 ounces salt cod,
  soaked (see page 4)
water, to cover salt cod
6 tablespoons olive oil, plus
  more to prepare baking dish
2 onions, thinly sliced
1 clove garlic, crushed

3 large waxy potatoes, boiled,
  peeled and thickly sliced
freshly ground black pepper
½ cup finely chopped fresh
  flat-leaf parsley, to serve
½ cup black olives marinated
  in oil, to serve

Drain the soaked cod, place in a saucepan, cover with fresh water and bring to a boil over medium heat. Reduce heat and simmer gently for 15 minutes, or until tender. Drain, allow to cool, then flake the fish, removing any bones or skin.

Preheat oven to 400°F. Lightly oil a baking dish.

Heat 2 tablespoons of the olive oil in a non-stick fry pan over medium heat. Add onions and sauté for 10–15 minutes, until soft and starting to caramelize. Add garlic and cook for an additional 2 minutes, then transfer pan contents to a plate and set aside.

While fry pan is still warm, heat half the remaining olive oil. Add sliced potatoes and sauté for about 5 minutes, turning once or twice, until they are lightly browned. >

Arrange half the potatoes on the bottom of the prepared baking dish, , top with flaked cod, then half the onions. Scatter with half of the chopped parsley, add a grind of black pepper, then repeat with remaining ingredients. Drizzle remaining olive oil over the top.

Bake in the preheated oven for 25 minutes. Scatter with the remaining parsley and olives, and serve.

✕ When choosing salt cod, remember that the narrow tail pieces will be saltier and have more bones – choose a middle piece for best results.

Clams in Fresh Tomato Sauce

SERVES 4

3 tablespoons olive oil
1 red onion, finely chopped
4 cloves garlic, chopped
2 pounds 3 ounces vine-ripened tomatoes, finely chopped
½ cup chopped fresh flat-leaf parsley

1 bay leaf (fresh if possible)
½ cup dry white wine or dry sherry, such as Chardonnay or Fino
2 pounds 3 ounces small clams, scrubbed
salt and freshly ground black pepper

Heat olive oil in a large heavy-based fry pan over medium heat. Add onion and garlic, and sauté for 2–3 minutes until softened. Add tomatoes and continue cooking for 5 minutes, stirring occasionally. Add parsley, bay leaf and wine or sherry, and simmer for 10 minutes until liquid has reduced into a sauce.

Add clams and increase heat. Cover and steam for 4–5 minutes, until shells open. (Discard any clams that do not open.)

Check sauce for seasoning and add salt and pepper to taste. Serve immediately.

Chickpeas with Tomatoes, Spinach & Almonds

SERVES 4

3 tablespoons olive oil

2 onions, chopped

2 cloves garlic, chopped

14 ounces canned chopped
   tomatoes

1 cup vegetable stock

a few saffron threads, crumbled

1 teaspoon hot Spanish
   paprika

½ cup sliced almonds,
   toasted and ground

14 ounces canned chickpeas,
   rinsed and drained

2 cups chopped baby spinach
   leaves

salt and freshly ground black
   pepper

Heat olive oil in a heavy-based, non-stick saucepan over medium heat. Add onions and garlic, and cook over a low heat, stirring occasionally, for 15–20 minutes until golden and beginning to caramelize.

Add tomatoes to pan and continue cooking for 15 minutes, until mixture becomes a thick sauce. Add stock, saffron, paprika, almonds and chickpeas, and cook for 15 minutes or until most of the liquid has evaporated. Stir chopped spinach through and cook until leaves wilt. Season to taste with salt and pepper. Serve hot or at room temperature.

Madrid Hotpot
Cocido Madrileno

SERVES 6

1 pound dried chickpeas,
   soaked overnight
water, to cover chickpeas
1 pound boneless beef shank
1 (2-pound) stewing chicken,
   cut into 8 pieces (see note
   page 173)
1/2 pound prosciutto or
   pancetta, diced
1 ham bone
5–6 cloves garlic
1 bay leaf
5–6 peppercorns,
   roughly crushed

3 large carrots,
   cut into large pieces
2 stalks celery,
   cut into large pieces
9 ounces medium-sized
   potatoes, quartered
½ pound fresh chorizo
   sausage, thickly sliced
salt and freshly ground black
   pepper
2 cups shredded cabbage

Drain chickpeas, place in a stockpot, add enough cold water to cover by about 2 inches, and bring to a boil. Skim off any scum.

Add the beef, chicken, prosciutto or pancetta, ham bone, garlic, bay leaf and peppercorns. Bring to simmering point, skim off any more scum that rises, cover, and simmer for 1 hour. (Add more water during cooking if needed – the liquid should always cover the ingredients). Add the carrots, celery, potatoes and chorizo to the pan, and season with salt and pepper. Cover and simmer for another 30 minutes.

When meat and vegetables are tender, stir in shredded cabbage and cook for a few more minutes until it wilts. Serve from the pot or, as is traditional in Spain, serve the broth as the first course, the vegetables as the second course, and the meat as the third course.

✕ If you can't buy a stewing chicken, you can use a roasting chicken. If so, add it after the meat has been simmering for 1 hour.

✕ Different regions have their own version of *cocido*; black pudding (*morcilla*) is a popular addition.

Rabbit with Pancetta & Thyme

SERVES 4

1 pound 10 ounces boned
   rabbit, cut into 8 even-sized
   pieces
2 cloves garlic, halved
salt and freshly ground black
   pepper
8 slices pancetta or thinly
   sliced bacon
3 tablespoons olive oil
1 pound 10 ounces
   vine-ripened tomatoes,
   peeled and chopped
2 tablespoons fresh thyme
   leaves

Preheat oven to 400°F.

Pat rabbit pieces dry with paper towels. Rub skin with garlic, then season all over with salt and pepper. Wrap a slice of pancetta or bacon around each piece of rabbit.

Heat olive oil in a medium-sized saucepan, add tomatoes and cook over low heat for 8–10 minutes, until they form a sauce. Stir in thyme, and season with a little salt and pepper.

Spoon tomato sauce over the bottom of an ovenproof casserole dish. Place rabbit bundles on top, in a single layer. Cover dish, place in preheated oven and bake for 40–50 minutes, basting occasionally, until meat is tender.

Serve hot.

Chicken with Sherry & Garlic

SERVES 4

2 tablespoons olive oil

1 (4-pound) chicken, cut into
8 pieces

salt and freshly ground black
pepper

1 tablespoon butter

1 pound 5 ounces small baby
potatoes, thickly sliced

2 heads of garlic, cloves
separated but not peeled

4 sprigs fresh tarragon

2 bay leaves, fresh if possible

½ cup medium–dry sherry

Preheat oven to 350°F.

Heat olive oil in a wide baking pan over medium heat on top of the stove. Season chicken pieces with salt and pepper, place in pan and cook for a few minutes on each side until golden brown. Transfer chicken to a plate.

Leave baking pan on stove, add butter, then add potato slices, garlic, tarragon and bay leaves, and toss to combine. Return chicken pieces to the pan in a single layer, skin-side up. Pour in sherry and bring to boiling point. Place baking pan in preheated oven and bake, uncovered, for 45–50 minutes, turning once or twice, until chicken is crisp and golden.

Quail Roasted in Vine Leaves

SERVES 4

oil, to prepare baking dish
8 quail
salt and freshly ground black
  pepper
1 tablespoon grated lemon zest
1–2 tablespoons fresh oregano
  leaves

3 tablespoons brandy
8 pieces thinly sliced jamon
  or bacon, rind removed
about 8 large preserved vine
  leaves, rinsed
3 tablespoons freshly squeezed
  lemon juice

Preheat oven to 400°F. Oil a baking dish that will hold the quail in one layer.

Rinse quail inside and out, and pat dry with paper towels. Season cavity with salt and pepper, lemon zest and oregano, and spoon in brandy.

Wrap a piece of ham or bacon around each quail, then wrap in a vine leaf (if vine leaves aren't large enough, you may need to use extra). Tie a piece of string around the quail, to secure.

Arrange quail in a single layer in the baking dish and place in preheated oven for about 15 minutes. To test if quail are cooked, insert a skewer into the flesh – the juices should run clear. **>**

Transfer quail to a warmed serving platter, remove string and keep warm. Pour lemon juice into a saucepan with the pan juices, stir to combine, and heat through.

Spoon sauce over quail and serve immediately.

※ If you prefer, you can use prosciutto instead of ham or bacon.

Oxtail Braised in Red Wine

SERVES 4

5½ pound oxtail, cut into
  2-inch lengths (ask the
  butcher to do this for you)
cold water, to rinse oxtail
salt and freshly ground black
  pepper
all-purpose flour, for dusting
¾ cup olive oil
2 brown onions, chopped
2 cloves garlic, chopped

2 carrots, chopped
2 stalks celery, chopped
2 tablespoons tomato paste
3 cups beef or veal stock
2 cups dry red wine
1 bay leaf
1 sprig fresh thyme
finely chopped fresh flat-leaf
  parsley, for garnish

Rinse oxtail in cold water, then pat dry with paper towels. Season with salt and pepper, dip into flour to coat, and shake off any excess.

Heat olive oil in a wide, heavy-based non-stick saucepan over medium–high heat. Add oxtail pieces in batches, sautéing for 5–6 minutes until lightly browned. As you finish each batch, set aside on a plate. If there is quite a lot of fat in the pan when you have finished, drain the fat, leaving just enough to fry the vegetables. ➤

Add onions, garlic, carrot and celery to saucepan and cook, stirring, for 10–12 minutes, until onion is lightly browned and vegetables softening. Return oxtail to the pan, add tomato paste, stock and wine. Stir to combine, then add bay leaf and thyme. Bring to simmering point, cover, reduce heat, and simmer for 2–2½ hours, until oxtail is very tender.

Remove oxtail pieces and place on a warmed serving dish. Remove bay leaf and discard. Purée remaining ingredients in a blender or food processor, then strain back into the pan. Check seasoning, reheat sauce and then spoon it over the oxtail. Scatter with parsley and serve hot.

✕ Creamy mashed potatoes are delicious with this, soaking up the rich sauce.

Pork Belly with Thyme & Red Wine

SERVES 4–6

salt

2 pounds 3 ounces pork belly

salt, to press onto pork rind

1 tablespoon olive oil

2 sprigs fresh thyme

2 tablespoons cumin seeds

RED-WINE SAUCE

2 tablespoons olive oil

1 small red onion, finely
    chopped

sprig fresh thyme

1 tablespoon red-wine vinegar

1 cup dry red wine

Press salt onto the pork rind about 1 hour before cooking (this absorbs some of the moisture).

Preheat oven to 425°F.

Scrape salt off the pork rind and pat dry with paper towels. Pour olive oil into an ovenproof dish and put in oven for a few minutes to heat. When olive oil is warm, place pork in the dish, rind down. Add thyme sprigs and scatter pork with cumin seeds.

Place pork in preheated oven and roast for 30 minutes. Reduce heat to 375°F and roast for another 30 minutes, then turn meat over and roast for 10–15 minutes more. ❯

To make the sauce, heat olive oil in a small saucepan over medium heat. Add onion and thyme, and sauté for 2–3 minutes until onion softens. Add vinegar and cook for 1 minute, then add wine and cook over medium–high heat for about 5 minutes until sauce reduces.

Remove pork from oven to a warmed dish, cover to keep warm and let rest at least 5–10 minutes. To serve, slice pork and spoon red-wine sauce over.

Sherry Chicken with Orange

SERVES 6

1 tablespoon olive oil

6 entire chicken legs, thigh
and drumstick

1 brown-skinned onion, finely
chopped

1 medium-sized carrot, finely
chopped

1 bay leaf

½ cup dry sherry

3 teaspoons finely grated
orange zest

¾ cup freshly squeezed orange
juice, strained

1 cup chicken stock

1 small orange, peeled,
pith removed and
flesh cut into cubes

1 cup pimento-stuffed green
olives, drained

Preheat oven to 350°F.

Heat olive oil in a large, heavy-based fry pan over medium–high heat and sauté
chicken in batches, for about 5–6 minutes, until golden brown. Transfer
chicken to a large roasting dish.

Pour excess fat from pan, leaving enough to sauté vegetables. Reduce heat,
add onion and sauté until softened and starting to brown. Add carrot and bay
leaf and cook, stirring occasionally, for about 5 minutes until softened.

Pour in sherry and cook for 1 minute, then add orange zest, orange juice and stock. Bring to a boil, stir well, and scrape up any bits that have stuck to the bottom of the pan. Pour sauce over the chicken, place dish in preheated oven and bake for about 1 hour, until chicken is cooked.

Remove dish from the oven, pour off juices into a small saucepan, cover chicken and keep warm. Skim any oil from surface of cooking juices, then bring cooking juices to a boil and simmer for 10 minutes until sauce thickens and reduces.

Pour sauce over chicken, then scatter orange cubes and olives on top. Return chicken to the oven, uncovered, and bake for about 5 minutes, or until orange cubes are is warmed through.

Saffron Chicken
with Garlic Picada

SERVES 4

3 pounds 5 ounces chicken,
   cut into 8 serving pieces
salt
2 teaspoons sweet Spanish
   paprika
1 teaspoon saffron threads
½ cup dry white wine
4 tablespoons olive oil

1 slice good-quality, day-old
   white bread, crusts
   removed, cut into cubes
8 cloves garlic, lightly crushed
¾ cup chicken or vegetable
   stock
salt and freshly ground black
   pepper

Pat chicken pieces dry with paper towels, then rub well with salt and paprika. Crumble saffron into the white wine and let soak.

Heat olive oil in a large, heavy-based non-stick fry pan over medium heat. Add bread cubes and fry until golden, then remove from pan and set aside. Add garlic to pan and sauté for 1–2 minutes, remove and set aside.

Add chicken pieces to pan and cook, turning occasionally, for about 10 minutes, until lightly browned all over. Add saffron-infused wine and the stock. Cover, reduce heat and simmer over very low heat for about 20 minutes.

Put garlic in a mortar with a little salt and plenty of black pepper, and pound. Gradually add the fried bread cubes and mash everything to a paste (you could do this in a food processor or blender). Add a little liquid from the fry pan to dilute the paste.

When chicken is almost cooked, stir in the garlic paste, and simmer for another 5 minutes until sauce thickens and chicken is cooked. Remove pan from the heat and let chicken stand for a few minutes before serving.

✕ If you prefer, buy chicken pieces on the bone, including some thighs for maximum flavor.

✕ A *picada* is a paste added to a dish towards the end of the cooking time, to boost aroma, flavor and texture. The ingredients vary but typically include garlic, oil, herbs, bread (toasted or fried) and nuts. Other flavorings, including herbs, may also be added.

Slow-cooked Lamb with Lemon

SERVES 4

2 pounds 3 ounces boneless
lamb shoulder, cut into
bite-sized cubes
salt and freshly ground black
pepper
2 tablespoons olive oil
1 onion, chopped
3 cloves garlic, crushed
1 tablespoon sweet Spanish
paprika

juice of 1 lemon
1 teaspoon grated lemon zest
½ cup finely chopped fresh
flat-leaf parsley
¾ cup chicken stock
salt and freshly ground black
pepper, to taste
extra chopped fresh flat-leaf
parsley and grated lemon
zest, for garnish

Season lamb with salt and pepper. Heat olive oil in a heavy-based, non-stick saucepan over medium heat. Add lamb in batches and sauté for 6–8 minutes until browned all over. Transfer cooked lamb to a plate.

In the same saucepan, sauté onion and garlic for about 5 minutes until softened. Add paprika, lemon juice and zest, parsley and stock, and stir. Return lamb pieces to the pan and bring to a boil. Reduce heat to very low, cover and simmer for 1–1½ hours, checking occasionally. When lamb is very tender, add salt and pepper to taste. Scatter with extra parsley and lemon zest, and serve hot.

Sweets

The Spanish definitely love their sweets — from crispy churros dipped in rich hot chocolate, to milky custards and a myriad of small cakes and biscuits.

The generous use of almonds and other nuts, plump figs, and spices such as cinnamon, nutmeg and cloves, are a reminder of the influence of the Arab world. The oranges and lemons that thrive in the Mediterranean climate add a citrus tang to many sweet treats.

< WALNUT PASTRY PUFFS (PAGE 194)

Walnut Pastry Puffs
Casadielles

MAKES 16

3½ ounces shelled walnuts, crushed

3 tablespoons superfine (bar) sugar

2 tablespoons anise liqueur (such as Anis del Mono, or sambuca)

2 tablespoons butter, melted

4 sheets pre-rolled, ready-to-bake puff pastry

1 egg white, lightly beaten

confectioner's (powdered) sugar, for garnish

Preheat oven to 425°F. Line a baking sheet with parchment (baking) paper.

Put walnuts, sugar, liqueur and melted butter in a small bowl and mix to combine.

Cut pastry into rectangles about 4½ inches × 2½ inches. Put a small spoonful of walnut mixture along the center of each pastry rectangle. Brush edges with egg white, then fold over pastry, joining long sides first, and press edges to seal. Place on baking sheet and bake in preheated oven for 15–20 minutes, until puffed and lightly browned.

Serve warm, dusted with confectioner's sugar.

※ Casadielles are puff pastry turnovers. Typically served at Christmas time in northern Spain, these fragrantly delicious mouthfuls are usually eaten warm. Make sure the walnuts are fresh, as stale ones can be bitter.

Almond & Chocolate Figs

SERVES 4

½ cup sliced almonds
1 ounce good quality dark
  chocolate, chopped
a few drops of amontillado, or
  other dry sherry
8 firm fresh figs
crème fraîche and cocoa
  powder, to serve (optional)

Place sliced almonds in a non-stick fry pan and cook over medium heat, stirring, for a few minutes, until they are lightly toasted.

Preheat oven to 350°F. Line a small baking dish with parchment (baking) paper.

Put toasted almonds, chocolate and sherry into food processor or blender and pulse until mixture has the consistency of breadcrumbs.

Remove stems from figs and cut a cross in the top of each. Push gently to open top of each fig and stuff with a small spoonful of the chocolate mixture. Gently pinch closed.

Place figs in baking dish and bake in preheated oven for 10–15 minutes until warmed through. Serve warm or at room temperature, with a small scoop of crème fraîche and a dusting of cocoa powder, if desired.

※ If you can find very plump dried figs, you could also use them to make this recipe.

Rice Pudding
Arroz con leche

SERVES 4

2 cups whole milk
1 cinnamon stick
1 strip lemon zest,
   about 2 inches long
a few drops of vanilla extract

½ cup short-grain rice
2 egg yolks, lightly beaten
3 ounces superfine (bar) sugar
4 tablespoons butter
ground cinnamon, to serve

Pour milk into a medium-sized saucepan, add cinnamon stick, lemon zest and vanilla extract, and heat just below boiling point. Strain milk, then return to saucepan. Add rice and egg yolks, and simmer over medium–low heat for 20 minutes, stirring gently to prevent the mixture sticking.

When rice is completely cooked, stir in superfine sugar and butter, and continue cooking for a few minutes.

Serve warm or at room temperature, sprinkled with ground cinnamon.

Figs with Oranges & Walnuts

SERVES 6

water, to cook figs
12 dried figs, stems removed
3 tablespoons honey
1 teaspoon finely grated lemon
  zest

1 cinnamon stick
3 oranges, peeled
½ cup walnuts, toasted
plain yoghurt or crème fraîche,
  to serve

Put figs, ½ cup water, honey, lemon zest and cinnamon stick in a saucepan. Place over medium heat and simmer gently for 15–20 minutes, stirring occasionally, until figs are soft. Set aside, and discard cinnamon stick.

Remove any pith from the oranges, cut flesh into thin slices and put in a bowl (collect any juice and add to the bowl). Add cooked figs and syrup to the bowl and stir gently to combine. Let cool, then chill in refrigerator.

Stir through the toasted walnuts and serve with plain yoghurt or crème fraîche.

Almond Lemon Cake

SERVES 8–10

4 eggs
5½ ounces superfine (bar) sugar
½ teaspoon ground cardamom
juice and finely grated zest of 1 lemon
few drops of vanilla extract

14 ounces ground almonds
confectioner's (powdered) sugar, for dusting
crème fraîche, to serve (optional)

Preheat oven to 375°F. Lightly grease an 8-inch round cake pan and line the bottom with parchment (baking) paper.

Beat eggs until light and fluffy. Add superfine sugar a few spoonfuls at a time, beating well after each addition, until mixture is thick and creamy. Fold in cardamom, lemon juice and zest, vanilla extract and ground almonds until mixed (do not beat).

Pour mixture into prepared cake pan. Bake in preheated oven for 35–40 minutes. When cake is ready, it will come away from sides of the tin and be firm to the touch in the center. Let stand for 10 minutes, then invert onto a cake rack to cool.

Serve dusted with confectioner's sugar, with a dollop of crème fraîche, if desired.

Spanish Doughnuts
Churros

SERVES 4

water
7 tablespoons butter
pinch of salt
1 cup all-purpose flour
3 eggs, lightly beaten
vegetable or olive oil
   for deep-frying

bread cube, to test oil
superfine (bar) sugar and
   ground cinnamon, for
   dusting (optional)

Put 1 cup water, butter and salt in a heavy-based saucepan over medium–high heat and bring to a boil. Pour in flour and beat with a wooden spoon until flour is completely mixed and dough forms a ball.

Let dough cool a little. Then add the beaten eggs, a little at a time, beating well after each addition, until combined. Spoon mix into a churro-maker or a piping bag with a large fluted nozzle.

Heat 1½–2 inches of oil in a heavy-based saucepan until very hot (350°F). To test, drop in a small cube of bread – it should sizzle and turn brown within 15 seconds. Reduce heat, then pipe 4-inch strips (or loops) directly into the oil. (Only cook 3 or 4 churros at a time, to keep the oil hot.) Deep-fry for a minute or so, turning once, until golden. **>**

Remove churros with a slotted spoon or tongs, and drain on paper towels. While still warm, dust with confectioner's sugar and cinnamon (if using). Serve with warm chocolate sauce (page 203), or hot chocolate for dipping.

✕ Churros are a classic Spanish breakfast treat, but make a delicious snack at any time. Churro-makers (*churreras*), designed for extruding the batter, are available from specialty cookware shops and Spanish food stores.

Chocolate Sauce

2 cups milk

2 teaspoons cornstarch

3½ ounces good-quality dark
   chocolate, chopped

3 tablespoons superfine (bar)
   sugar

pinch ground cinnamon

Pour about a quarter of the milk into a small bowl, add cornstarch and whisk to combine. Set aside.

Pour remaining milk into a medium-sized saucepan over low heat, add chocolate and stir until chocolate has melted. Add milk/cornstarch mix, sugar and cinnamon, and continue stirring over low heat for another 5 minutes until mixture thickens.

Serve warm as a dipping sauce for churros (page 201), or with ice-cream.

Catalan Cream
Crema Catalana

SERVES 6

1 quart 2 ounces whole milk
1 vanilla pod, split open
1 tablespoon cornstarch
6 egg yolks

7 ounces superfine (bar) sugar
extra 4 tablespoons superfine
sugar, for toffee crust

Put milk in a medium-sized saucepan with vanilla pod over medium heat and bring slowly to a boil. Remove from the heat and let infuse for 1 hour, then strain and let cool.

Mix cornstarch with 3 tablespoons of the cooled milk. Beat egg yolks with the superfine sugar until pale, then stir in the cornstarch mixture. Add the egg mixture to the remaining cooled milk, place over medium heat and cook, stirring, until the custard thickens. Pour into individual ovenproof dishes and refrigerate until ready to serve.

To serve, sprinkle superfine sugar in a thin layer on top of each custard and place under a very hot broiler (or use a kitchen blowtorch) until a toffee crust forms.

✕ For a modern spin on this creamy dessert, add the finely grated zest of 1 lime to the milk instead of the vanilla pod.

Coffee Liqueur Flan

SERVES 6–8

¾ cup superfine(bar) sugar
1 (14-ounce) can sweetened
 condensed milk
1 quart whole milk
5 eggs
1 tablespoon strong espresso
 coffee

1 tablespoon coffee liqueur
pinch of salt
boiling water, to fill outer pan
heavy cream, to serve
 (optional)

Preheat oven to 350°F.

Put superfine sugar in a small, heavy-based saucepan over medium heat and leave it, without stirring, until sugar starts to melt. Then stir occasionally until it melts completely and turns a light golden color. Pour it into a 9-inch cake pan and turn pan so caramel covers the bottom. (Take care, as the caramel is very hot). Allow to set.

Put remaining ingredients in a blender or food processor and blend until smooth. Pour mixture through a fine sieve over the caramel bottom. Cover loosely with aluminum foil. **>**

Place cake pan in a larger baking pan, at least 2-inches deep. Pour boiling water into the outer pan to a depth of about 1 inch, then carefully place pan in preheated oven and bake for 1–1¼ hours. The custard is ready when it is set, but still moves gently, and a knife inserted in the center comes out clean. Remove from oven and allow to cool completely. Transfer to refrigerator and chill overnight or for at least 8 hours.

To remove flan from pan, run a knife carefully around the edge to loosen. Place a large platter over the pan, then carefully invert, holding pan and platter together. The caramel will form a sauce over the flan.

Serve chilled, with heavy cream if desired.

Seville Oranges with Cinnamon Wine Syrup

3 cups light red wine
   (tempranillo or beaujolais
   are good)
1 cup superfine (bar) sugar
1 cinnamon stick
3 cloves
finely grated zest of ½ orange
6 oranges

Put wine, superfine sugar, cinnamon stick, cloves and orange zest in a saucepan and stir over medium heat until sugar dissolves. Bring to a boil, and boil uncovered for about 15 minutes until the liquid reduces to a syrup. Allow to cool, then cover and refrigerate. (Syrup can be made a day ahead.)

Peel oranges and remove all pith and membranes. Using a very sharp knife, cut oranges into segments, saving any juice. Divide segments and juice among serving bowls.

Spoon chilled syrup over the orange segments, and serve.

Spanish Cakes
Magdalenas

MAKES 24

3 cups all-purpose flour
1 teaspoon baking powder
pinch of salt
1 large egg,
   at room temperature
1¼ cups superfine (bar) sugar

1 tablespoon finely grated
   lemon zest
1 cup milk
1 cup light olive oil
confectioner's (powdered)
   sugar, for dusting

Preheat oven to 350°F. Arrange paper cupcake liners on a baking sheet, or lightly grease a cupcake pan.

Sift flour with baking powder and salt. Beat egg, superfine sugar and lemon zest until pale and fluffy. Gradually fold in milk, olive oil and sifted flour mixture, well after each addition.

Spoon mixture into paper cupcake liners or cupcake pan, filling about two-thirds full. Place in preheated oven and bake for 15 minutes, until puffed and golden.

Transfer to a cake rack to cool. Dust with confectioner's sugar to serve.

✕ Magdalenas are small, light and fluffy, sweet and rich-tasting cakes, traditionally eaten at breakfast.

Fig Roll
Pan de higo

SERVES 8–10

1 pound 10 ounces dried figs
  (stems removed), chopped
½ cup blanched almonds,
  toasted and chopped
½ cup hazelnuts,
  toasted and chopped
1 tablespoon sesame seeds,
  lightly toasted
1½ tablespoons confectioner's
  (powdered) sugar

1 teaspoon ground cinnamon
¼ teaspoon ground cloves
1 tablespoon brandy, plus
  more to hold mixture
  together
2 ounces good-quality dark
  chocolate, melted
extra confectioner's sugar,
  (optional)

Put chopped figs, almonds, hazelnuts, sesame seeds, confectioner's sugar, cinnamon and cloves in a food processor or blender and process until mixture starts to come together. It will be sticky, but should have some texture.

Put the mixture into a bowl and stir in brandy and melted chocolate until mixture is quite stiff and sticky. Add a little more brandy if it is not holding together.

Lay two sheets of aluminum foil or parchment (baking) paper on the work surface and sprinkle with confectioner's sugar. ❯

Shape mixture into two small logs and roll up each one tightly in a sheet of the foil or paper. Twist ends to secure. Store in a cool place, or refrigerate, for at least 2 days before serving.

To serve, bring logs back to room temperature and use a sharp knife to cut into slices.

Dust with extra confectioner's sugar if desired.

✕ This delectable sweet is perfect served with a strong coffee or an Amontillado sherry, or as part of a cheese platter.

Fried Milk

Leche frita

SERVES 6

3 cups whole milk
1 strip lemon zest,
   2-inches long
1 cinnamon stick
1⅔ sticks butter
½ cup all-purpose flour
6½ ounces superfine (bar)
   sugar

6 egg yolks
1 egg, whisked
2 cups fine dry breadcrumbs
vegetable oil for deep-frying
confectioner's (powdered)
   sugar and ground
   cinnamon, to serve

Lightly oil an 8-inch square baking pan.

Put milk, lemon zest and cinnamon stick in a saucepan over medium–high heat. Bring to a boil, then reduce heat and simmer for 5 minutes. Remove from heat, cover to keep warm and let infuse for 5 minutes, then strain. Discard lemon zest and cinnamon stick.

In another saucepan, melt butter over low heat. Add flour and cook, stirring constantly, for 5 minutes. Take pan off the heat, slowly pour in the warm milk mixture, whisking to mix. Add sugar and whisk again, then return to low heat and stir continuously until mixture thickens and coats the spoon. >

Remove mixture from heat and gradually whisk in egg yolks. Return pan to heat and continue stirring until mixture forms a thick custard. Pour the custard into prepared baking pan, smooth the surface, cover, and refrigerate overnight.

When ready to serve, cut the custard into 8 squares, or small triangles if you prefer. Dip custard pieces into egg, then into breadcrumbs, to coat lightly.

Heat about 1 inch of vegetable oil into a large, deep fry pan until hot. Fry custard pieces in batches, turning once, for 3–4 minutes. Drain on paper towels.

Dust with confectioner's sugar and ground cinnamon, and serve warm or at room temperature.

Custard Tarts

MAKES 12

8 ounces superfine(bar) sugar
½ cup water
1½ tablespoons cornstarch
2 cups milk
½ cup heavy cream

3 egg yolks, lightly beaten
oil, to prepare muffin pan
3 sheets pre-rolled ready-to-
   bake butter puff pastry

Place superfine sugar and ½ cup water in a saucepan over medium–high heat. Cook, stirring, for 2–3 minutes until sugar dissolves. Bring to boil and boil, without stirring, for 3 minutes, to make a syrup. Let cool.

Put cornstarch in a bowl and gradually add milk, stirring until combined. Add heavy cream and mix well again. Whisk in the egg yolks, then add sugar syrup and whisk again until combined.

Pour mixture into a clean saucepan and cook over medium heat, stirring, until custard comes just to a boil. Remove from heat and set aside to cool.

Preheat oven to 425°F. Lightly oil a 12-cup, non-stick muffin pan, or 12 individual small tart pans. ❯

Cut pastry into 3-inch rounds. Press pastry into oiled muffin pan and prick the bottoms with a fork. Spoon in the custard, half-filling the pastry shells.. Place on top rack of preheated oven and bake for 15–20 minutes until pastry is golden.

Remove tarts from oven, let cool in pans for a few minutes, then transfer to a cooling rack.

Serve warm or at room temperature, preferably on the day they are made.

※ Some dark spots will appear on the pastry and custard as the tarts cook: this is quite traditional.

※ The custard will sink a little as the tarts cool.

Peaches Poached in Red Wine

4 ripe white peaches
boiling water and ice water, to
    cover peaches
water, to cook peaches
1½ cups dry red wine
½ cup superfine (bar) sugar
1 cinnamon stick

1 tablespoon freshly squeezed
    lemon juice
1 teaspoon grated lemon zest
cream or ice cream, to serve
    (optional)

Put peaches in a bowl or saucepan, cover with boiling water and leave for 30 seconds. Transfer peaches to a bowl of ice water, leave for another 30 seconds, then remove and peel off skins (they should slip off easily).

Put wine, 1½ cups water, sugar, cinnamon stick, lemon juice and zest in a saucepan and stir to mix. Add peeled peaches in a single layer. Place saucepan over medium heat and bring to a simmer. Cover and simmer for 15 minutes.

Use a slotted spoon to transfer peaches to a serving bowl.

Bring the liquid in the saucepan to a boil and boil for a few minutes until it reduces to a syrup. Pour syrup over peaches and let cool. Refrigerate until well chilled.

Serve chilled, with cream or ice cream, if desired.

✕ You can substitute pears for the peaches. Lightly toast a handful of slivered almonds to sprinkle over the fruit before serving.

Almond Biscuits

Polvorones

4 ounces blanched almonds, lightly toasted

4½ ounces butter, at room temperature

5 ounces superfine sugar

½ teaspoon vanilla extract

generous pinch of ground cinnamon

8 ounces all-purpose flour, sifted

confectioner's (powdered) sugar, for dusting

Preheat oven to 250°F. Line a baking sheet with parchment (baking) paper. Put almonds in a blender or food processor and process until finely ground.

Beat butter, superfine sugar, vanilla extract and cinnamon together until pale and creamy. Use a spoon to beat in the flour and ground almonds, until soft and crumbly. Take a walnut-sized ball of the mixture and place on the prepared baking sheet. Press gently to form small disc about ¾-inch thick. Repeat with remaining mixture, leaving plenty of space between each biscuit.

Place in preheated oven and bake for 25 minutes (they should still be quite pale). Allow to cool completely before transferring carefully from the sheet: use a spatula, as they break very easily). Dust generously with confectioner's sugar before serving.

✕ Polvorones are Spanish shortbread. A special treat at Christmas time, *polvorones* are traditionally made with lard, but this buttery version has the same delicate, crumbly texture and is just as delicious.

Raspberry & Cava Sorbet

SERVES 4

½ cup superfine (bar) sugar
water, to make syrup
12 ounces fresh raspberries,
　rinsed
1 cup freshly squeezed orange
　juice

1 cup brut cava or other dry
　sparkling wine
fresh berries, for garnish

Stir sugar and 3 tablespoons water in a small saucepan over medium–low heat until sugar dissolves. Pour syrup into a bowl.

Purée raspberries in a food processor or blender, then strain purée to remove seeds. Add purée to sugar syrup, then stir in orange juice and cava. Cover and refrigerate until chilled.

Pour raspberry mixture into an ice-cream maker and follow manufacturer's instructions. When sorbet is ready, transfer to a container and freeze.

Serve in chilled glasses with a mixture of fresh berries.

※ If you don't have an ice-cream maker, pour into a small baking pan and freeze, stir with a fork every few hours until amost frozen solid.

Valencia Cake with Orange Glaze

SERVES 8

1 cup freshly squeezed orange
   juice
2 teaspoons grated orange zest
a few threads of saffron,
   crumbled
2 cups all-purpose flour
pinch of salt
1½ teaspoons baking powder
1 cup superfine (bar) sugar
1 whole egg and 1 egg white
½ cup thick plain yogurt
3 tablespoons olive oil

GLAZE
1 tablespoon orange
   marmalade
2 teaspoons orange liqueur,
   such as Cointreau or Grand
   Marnier

Preheat oven to 350°F. Lightly grease a 10-inch cake pan and line the bottom
with parchment (baking) paper.

Warm the orange juice, add orange zest and saffron, and let soak for 10
minutes. Meanwhile, sift the flour with the salt and baking powder into a small
bowl.

Put sugar, whole egg and the egg white in a mixing bowl and beat at medium speed until thick and pale. Add yogurt and beat to combine. Add olive oil and saffron-infused orange juice and beat again. Gradually fold in sifted flour until mixed.

Spoon batter into prepared cake pan. Bake in preheated oven for 40 minutes, or until a skewer inserted in center comes out clean. Cake should be lightly browned and just coming away from the sides.

Let stand for 10 minutes, then invert on a wire rack. When cool, place on serving platter.

To make glaze, put marmalade and liqueur in a small saucepan over medium heat. Simmer, stirring, until melted together. Strain over cake, and serve.

Almond Meringues
Soplillos

MAKES ABOUT 30–36

5 ounces sliced almonds,
   lightly toasted and finely
   chopped
3 egg whites
pinch of salt
7 ounces superfine (bar) sugar
1 teaspoon freshly squeezed
   lemon juice

1–2 drops vanilla extract
2 teaspoons finely grated
   lemon zest
whipped cream,
   to serve (optional)

Preheat oven to 250°F. Line a mini-muffin pan with paper mini-cupcake liners.

Put egg whites in a clean, dry bowl with the salt, and whisk until stiff. Add superfine sugar gradually, a spoonful at a time, beating after each addition. When mixture is thick and glossy, beat in lemon juice and vanilla extract. Then carefully fold in the lemon zest and almonds.

Spoon mixture into paper mini-cupcake liners. Place in preheated oven and bake for 30 minutes, then turn off oven and let meringues dry out (1–2 hours). If the meringues start to brown, cover with a sheet of parchment (baking) paper.

Serve plain or with whipped cream, if desired.

✕ If you prefer, you can make the meringues without paper mini-cupcake liners and simply spoon the mixture into small piles on parchment paper.

St James Cake
Torta de Santiago

SERVES 8

4½ ounces all-purpose flour, sifted, plus flour to roll dough

2 tablespoons superfine (bar) sugar

½ teaspoon ground cinnamon

7 tablespoons cold butter, chopped

1 egg yolk, lightly beaten

FILLING

3 eggs

3½ ounces superfine sugar

8 ounces finely ground almonds

2 tablespoons finely grated lemon zest

2 tablespoons sweet sherry

confectioner's (powdered) sugar, for dusting

Preheat oven to 400°F. Lightly grease an 8-inch non-stick tart pan with removable bottom.

To make the dough, put flour, superfine sugar, cinnamon, butter and egg yolk in a food processor and process until the mixture forms a dough. Roll dough into a ball, cover and refrigerate for 30 minutes.

Roll out dough on a lightly floured surface and use to line tart pan. Press into place, trim edges and prick the dough with a fork. ➤

To make filling, whip eggs and superfine sugar until frothy, then fold in almonds, lemon zest and sherry. Pour into tart shell and smooth the surface.

Place tart in preheated oven and bake for 50 minutes. Remove from oven and leave in pan to cool.

When cool, transfer tart to a serving dish and dust top with confectioner's sugar.

✖ There are many variations of this cake, some with pastry on the bottom and some without, but all have almonds and the tang of lemons.

✖ The northern Spanish custom is to dust the confectioner's sugar around a stencil shape of the cross of the Order of Santiago.

Little Doughnut Rings
Rosquillos

SERVES 4

3 cups all-purpose flour, plus
   flour for forming ropes
1 teaspoon baking powder
7 fluid ounces milk
1 egg, beaten
3½ fluid ounces olive oil
1 teaspoon finely grated lemon
   zest

¼ teaspoon finely ground
   cinnamon
olive or vegetable oil for frying
½ teaspoon extra ground
   cinnamon mixed with
   superfine (bar) sugar,
   to serve

Sift flour and baking powder into a large bowl.

Mix milk, egg, olive oil, lemon zest and cinnamon in a second bowl and stir well. Add to flour mixture and mix until a soft dough forms (add a little extra flour if it seems too moist). Knead mixture for about 1 minute, then roll out on a lightly floured surface, to form ropes about ⁵⁄₈-inch thick and 6-inches long. Join ends to form a ring or doughnut shape.

Heat oil in a heavy-based fry pan or deep-fryer until hot (350°F). Add dough rings a few at a time, and cook for 3–4 minutes, turning once, until golden. Drain on paper towels. Let cool, then dip into the superfine sugar and cinnamon mix.

✕ Rosquillos are from the Spanish word "rosca" which means ringlet.

Custard Cream
Natillas

SERVES 4

4 eggs
1 quart 2 ounces whole milk
¾ cup superfine (bar) sugar
3 teaspoons cornstarch
finely grated zest of 1 lemon

1 cinnamon stick
ground cinnamon,
    for dusting (optional)

Beat eggs with 1 cup of the milk, superfine sugar and cornstarch, until frothy.

Put remaining milk in a heavy-based saucepan with lemon zest and cinnamon stick, and bring just to a boil. Remove from heat, and discard cinnamon stick.

Put saucepan back over a low heat and gradually add egg mixture, stirring all the time, until the custard thickens (about 10 minutes).

Allow custard to cool a little, then pour into a large serving bowl or individual small bowls. Chill for a few hours or overnight.

Dust lightly with ground cinnamon, if desired, before serving.

✕ Natillas is a cinnamon-flavored egg custard without the caramel sauce that tops flan.

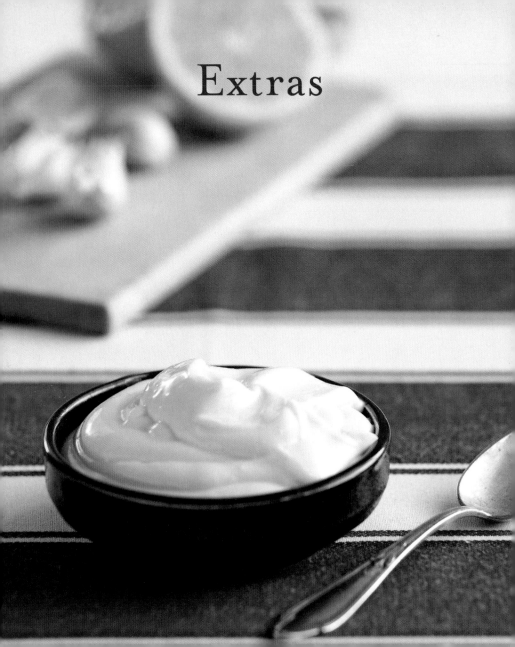

Extras

In many cases, a generous drizzle of Spain's renowned olive oil is all the sauce that accompanies a dish. But there are a few classic sauces that you might like to include in your repertoire.

It is definitely worth mastering alioli, a garlic-drenched mayonnaise especially typical of the Catalan region. It is often scooped onto fried potatoes, or used to add peppery creaminess to a fish stew or paella.

Bell peppers and other peppers — and olives, of course — also feature in a range of traditional accompaniments, such as the smoky, piquant romesco sauce.

‹ ALIOLI (PAGE 238)

Alioli

MAKES 1½ CUPS

3 cloves garlic, crushed
2 teaspoons salt flakes
(delicate finishing salt)
2 egg yolks, lightly beaten
1 cup extra-virgin olive oil
1 tablespoon freshly squeezed
lemon juice

Pound garlic and salt in a mortar until until a thick paste forms. Add egg yolks and mix until combined.

Pour garlic, salt and egg mixture into a food processor or blender. With the processor on, add the olive oil in a thin, slow, steady stream until a very thick mayonnaise forms. Stir in lemon juice. Adjust seasoning.

Keep, covered, in the refrigerator, until serving, to allow the flavors to develop.

※ A traditional alioli includes no eggs, only garlic and oil, but can be a little too potent for many tastes. A pinch of Spanish paprika can also be added. If short of time, use a good-quality egg mayonnaise and stir through some crushed garlic.

Green Sauce
Mojo verde

¾ cup extra-virgin olive oil

3 green habanero chili peppers, deseeded and finely chopped

2 cloves garlic, chopped

1 spring onion or scallion, finely chopped

1 tablespoon finely chopped fresh cilantro

1 teaspoon ground cumin

1 tablespoon white-wine vinegar

salt and freshly ground black pepper

Put all the ingredients in a food processor or blender and pulse to a thick paste. Alternatively, you can pound everything, except the olive oil, in a mortar. When you have a thick paste, slowly add the olive oil to make a sauce.

Cover and refrigerate until needed. Serve with grilled fish, seafood or chicken.

Romesco Sauce

4 ounces raw almonds

4 ounces raw hazelnuts

2 large red bell peppers, deseeded and thickly sliced

1/3 cup olive oil

4 cloves garlic, sliced

2 slices stale white bread (crusts removed), cut into cubes

2 medium-sized, vine-ripened tomatoes, peeled and chopped

1 teaspoon ground sweet Spanish paprika

2 tablespoons red-wine vinegar

salt and freshly ground black pepper

Preheat oven to 350°F.

Put almonds and hazelnuts on a baking sheet, place in preheated oven and bake for 5–10 minutes until they are lightly toasted and fragrant. Allow to cool, then rub to remove the skins. Roughly chop the nuts.

Put red bell pepper slices on a baking sheet, drizzle with 1 tablespoon of the olive oil and roast for 15–20 minutes, or until softened. Let cool.

Heat olive oil in a non-stick fry pan over medium heat until hot. Add garlic and sauté for 1–2 minutes. Add bread cubes and cook for another minute or so, until lightly browned. Remove to a plate to cool.

Add tomatoes to the pan and cook for 5 minutes until softened.

Put roasted red bell pepper slices, garlic, fried bread cubes, tomatoes, nuts, paprika and vinegar in a food processor or blender and process until mixture is thick. Season with salt and pepper to taste. Store in refrigerator (for up to 2 days), but serve at room temperature.

※ This piquant, bright-red sauce has innumerable variations and uses. It is delicious served as a dip with crusty bread, or a sauce for seafood or vegetables. You can thin it with a little water if needed.

Spanish Tapenade

MAKES 1¾ CUPS

1½ cups pitted black Spanish
    olives
8–10 anchovy fillets in oil,
    drained
2 tablespoons capers, rinsed

½ cup extra-virgin olive oil
finely grated zest of 1 lemon
sprig of fresh thyme
freshly ground black pepper

Place all the ingredients in a blender or food processor and pulse until mixed but still with some texture. Check for seasoning and add extra pepper if needed, and extra-virgin olive oil if mixture is a little dry.

Store, covered, in refrigerator, but serve at room temperature. Try it piled on slices of toasted baguette as a quick, flavorsome tapa.

✕ This chunky paste is a Mediterranean favorite. It can be served (as above) as a tapa, with grilled chicken or fish, or as a dip with spring or summer vegetables.

Roasted Red Bell Pepper

SERVES 4–6

4 red bell peppers,
  deseeded and quartered
3 tablespoons olive oil
1 tablespoon red-wine vinegar
1 clove garlic, crushed
1 spring onion or scallion,
  finely sliced

1 tablespoon chopped fresh
  flat-leaf parsley
pinch sweet Spanish paprika
salt and freshly ground black
  pepper

Preheat oven to 400°F.

Place red bell peppers on a baking tray, drizzle with a little of the olive oil and roast in preheated oven for about 20 minutes, until softened and just starting to blacken around the edges. (Alternatively, you can grill or barbecue the red bell peppers.)

Place cooked red bell peppers in a bowl and cover with food wrap to cool. When cool, peel off the skin, slice into strips and set aside.

Mix remaining olive oil with the vinegar, garlic, onion, parsley and paprika, and season with salt and pepper. Pour this marinade over the roasted red bell pepper slices, stir to coat and leave for at least a few hours for flavors to develop. (They will keep, covered in the refrigerator, for several days.) >

Bring the roasted red bell peppers slices to room temperature before serving – they are excellent served on a crusty tostado, but also go well with fish, grilled or barbecued meats, and in paellas and tortillas.

✕ You can buy roasted red bell peppers (loose, or in jars) from good delis and most supermarkets, but they are easy to prepare at home, and the flavor is worth it.

Sherry Vinaigrette

MAKES 1 CUP

¼ cup sherry vinegar
¾ cup extra-virgin olive oil
1 clove garlic, crushed
½ teaspoon salt

Whisk together the vinegar, olive oil and garlic until combined. Season with a little salt.

Store, covered, in refrigerator, but allow to return to room temperature before using.

Special Ingredients

CAVA Spanish sparkling wine, made by the traditional Champagne method. The generic term *cava* (cave) reflects the original tradition of aging the wine in underground cellars. Brut (dry) cava is recommended; if you can't find it, use any dry sparkling wine.

CHORIZO A pork sausage which gets its distinctive red color from *pimenton* (Spanish paprika). There are numerous regional varieties of chorizo – smoked or unsmoked, mild or hot, with or without garlic and spices. Chorizo is available both cured (ready to eat) and fresh (which must be cooked before eating).

JAMON Cured ham; a Spanish specialty of which there are many regional variations. The best-known and most readily available is the dry-cured jamon serrano. The most highly-prized variety (and also the most expensive) is jamon Iberico, made from the flesh of acorn-fed, black Iberian pigs. If you are unable to buy jamon, you could substitute prosciutto.

MANCHEGO A semi-firm Spanish cheese made from sheep milk. If it is not available you could use gruyere or Swiss cheese.

PAELLA RICE For the very best results use a classic Spanish short-grain variety as grown in Calasparra. Bomba rice is the finest of these short grain varieties, as it can absorb three times its volume in liquid while still retaining its shape. If you cannot buy Spanish rice, arborio is an acceptable substitute.

PIMIENTO In Spanish, 'pimiento' refers to all sweet peppers of the bell pepper family. Ranging from small to large, completely mild to extremely hot, pimientos come in red, green and yellow, and are an essential ingredient in much of Spanish cooking. Varieties popular in Spain include:

> **PADRON** Small, green, and somewhat sweet; these peppers are mainly mild but notoriously, about one in ten is extremely hot!

> **PIQUILLO** Small red peppers which are charred over coals, peeled, and bottled or canned with olive oil and herbs. Available at specialty food outlets, Spanish delicatessens and some supermarkets.

RIOJA Wine from La Rioja province in Spain. Rioja is aged in oak barrels and can be red (*tinto*), white (*blanco*) or rosé (*rosado*).

SHERRY (*vino de Jerez*) A fortified wine made from white grapes grown near the Jerez region in Spain. Sherry is made in a variety of styles, from the light dry wines known as *fino*, to the rich, sweet dessert wines such as Pedro Ximenez.

SPANISH PAPRIKA (*pimenton*) An essential ingredient in Spanish cuisine, adding color, spice and pungency, Spanish paprika is made from ripe, red pimientos that have been, dried, smoked and ground, and has a distinctive, strong smoky taste. Spanish paprika is available in sweet (*dulce*), mild (*agridulce*) and hot (*picante*) varieties.

VALDEON A rich, creamy Spanish blue cheese similar to roquefort.

Index

PENGUIN BOOKS

Published by the Penguin Group
Penguin Group (USA) Inc., 375 Hudson Street, New York, NY 10014, U.S.A
Penguin Group (Canada), 90 Eglinton Avenue East, Suite 700, Toronto, Ontario, Canada M4P 2Y3 (a division of Pearson
Penguin Canada Inc.)
Penguin Books Ltd, 80 Strand, London WC2R 0RL, England
Penguin Ireland, 25 St Stephen's Green, Dublin 2, Ireland (a division of Penguin Book Ltd)
Penguin Group (Australia), 250 Camberwell Road, Camberwell, Victoria 3124, Australia (a division of Pearson Australia
Group PTY Ltd)
Penguin Books India Pvt Ltd, 11 Community Centre, Panchsheel Park, New Delhi – 110 017, India
Penguin Group (NZ), 67 Apollo Drive, Rosedale, North Shore 0632,
New Zealand (a division of Pearson New Zealand Ltd)
Penguin Books (South Africa) (Pty) Ltd, 24 Sturdee Avenue, Rosebank, Johannesburg 2196, South Africa

Penguin Books Ltd, Registered Offices: 80 Strand, London, WC2R 0RL, England

First published by Penguin Group (Australia), 2010
This edition published in 2012 by Penguin Group (USA) Inc.

ISBN: 978-0-14-320298-1

Special Markets ISBN: 978-0-14-219664-9

10 9 8 7 6 5 4 3 2 1

Text and photographs copyright © Penguin Group (Australia), 2010

Designed by Marley Flory and Nikki Townsend © Penguin Group (Australia)
Photography by Julie Renouf
Food styling by Lee Blaylock
Typeset by Post Pre-press Group, Brisbane, Queensland
Scans and separations by Splitting Image, P/L, Clayton, Victoria

Printed in the United States of America